G's Daily
Prayers
and
Encouragements

G's Daily
Prayers
and
Encouragements

Prayer Changes Things

CALVIN C. GORDON

WESTBOW
PRESS®
A DIVISION OF THOMAS NELSON
& ZONDERVAN

WestBow Press books may be ordered through booksellers or by contacting:

WestBow Press
A Division of Thomas Nelson & Zondervan
1663 Liberty Drive
Bloomington, IN 47403
www.westbowpress.com
1 (866) 928-1240

ISBN: 978-1-9736-5984-6 (sc)
ISBN: 978-1-9736-5986-0 (hc)
ISBN: 978-1-9736-5985-3 (e)

Library of Congress Control Number: 2019905012

Print information available on the last page.

WestBow Press rev. date: 4/25/2019

JANUARY 1

Joy of Life

Consider it pure joy, my brothers and sisters, whenever you face
trials of many kinds, because you know that the testing of your
faith produces perseverance. Let perseverance finish its work so
that you may be mature and complete, not lacking anything.

—JAMES 1:2–4 (NIV)

Look to this day, for it is life, the very life of life.
In its brief course lie all the realities and verities of existence.
The bliss of growth, the splendor of action, the glory of power.
And yesterday is but a dream, and tomorrow is only a vision.
But today—well lived—makes every yesterday
a dream of happiness,
and every tomorrow a vision of hope.
Look well, therefore, to this day.

—SANSKRIT PROVERB

Dear God, thank you for moments of trials—times when we
earn our salaries. We know these moments are building strong
muscles within us and are precursors to a coming reward. Amen.

JANUARY 2

Peace and Understanding

And the peace of God, which transcends all understanding,
will guard your hearts and your minds in Christ Jesus.
—PHILIPPIANS 4:7 (NIV)

Communication will bring understanding and
understanding will cause harmonious mutual
relationships which can establish peace and stability.
—LOBSANG TENZIN

Dear God, we thank you for this day. We are praying
for peace in our families, communities, country, and
this world as a whole. Have mercy on us all. Amen.

JANUARY 3

Wisdom

If any of you lacks wisdom, you should ask God, who gives
generously to all without finding fault, and it will be given to you.

—JAMES 1:5 (NIV)

Talent is God-given. Be humble. Fame is man-given.
Be grateful. Conceit is self-given. Be careful.

—JOHN WOODEN

Dear God, we thank you again for another day. We pray to
be wise today and not allow ourselves to be foolish in our
actions and dealings with others. We love you. Amen.

JANUARY 4

Courage

Be strong and courageous. Do not be afraid or terrified
because of them, for the Lord your God goes with
you; he will never leave you nor forsake you.
—DEUTERONOMY 31:6 (NIV)

Don't believe what your eyes are telling you.
All they show is limitation.
Look with your understanding,
find out what you already know,
and you'll see the way to fly.
—RICHARD BACH

Dear God, we thank you for giving us the courage
to open our eyes to see the things you desire for us,
even when we don't fully understand. Amen.

JANUARY 5

Hope

❧

But God will never forget the needy; the hope
of the afflicted will never perish.
—PSALM 9:18 (NIV)

Stay positive and happy. Work hard and don't give up
hope. Be open to criticism and keep learning. Surround
yourself with happy, warm, and genuine people.
—TENA DESAE

Dear God, we thank you once again for this wonderful day.
We thank you for giving us hope and insight into what's going
on in this world. We know you are still in charge. Amen.

Pleasant

How good and pleasant it is when God's
people live together in unity!
—PSALM 133:1 (NIV)

God is ethics and morality: God is fearlessness. God is the
source of Light and Life and yet He is above and beyond all
these. God is conscience … He is a personal God to those
who need His personal presence. He is embodied to those
who need His touch. He is the purest essence. He simply
is to those who have faith. He is all things to all men.
—MAHATMA GANDHI

Dear Lord, make our words pleasant. Let them not
just instruct or reprove but bring sweetness and
health to all we encounter today. Amen.

JANUARY 7

Promise

For no matter how many promises God has made,
they are "Yes" in Christ. And so through him the
"Amen" is spoken by us to the glory of God.

—2 CORINTHIANS 1:20 (NIV)

The best and most beautiful things in the world
cannot be seen nor touched
but are felt in the heart.

—HELEN KELLER

Dear God, thank you for the new morning and the promise it
brings. Invigorate us today so we can know its blessings. Amen.

JANUARY 8

Confidence

So do not throw away your confidence; it will be richly rewarded.
—HEBREWS 10:35 (NIV)

At any moment
I could start being a better person ...
But, which moment should I choose?
—ASHLEIGH BRILLIANT, AUTHOR AND ARTIST

Dear God, help us walk carefully now so that others
can walk confidently in our footsteps later. Amen.

JANUARY 9

Power

For the kingdom of God is not a matter of talk but of power.
—1 CORINTHIANS 4:20 (NIV)

Trials are but lessons
that you failed to learn,
presented once again.
So, where you made a faulty choice before,
you can now make a better one,
and thus escape all pain
that what you chose before has brought to you.
—*A COURSE IN MIRACLES*

Dear God, let us never grow so hungry for power that it
becomes the thing we praise. Let power come and let power
go while our minds are forever fixed on you. Amen.

Unexpected

Moreover, no one knows when their hour will come: As fish are
caught in a cruel net, or birds are taken in a snare, so people
are trapped by evil times that fall unexpectedly upon them.

—ECCLESIASTES 9:12 (NIV)

Adversity has the effect of eliciting talents which, in
prosperous circumstances, would have lain dormant.

—HORACE, 65–68 BC

Dear God, thank you for the unexpected. Our eyes are
open to see bright lights in new spaces. Amen.

JANUARY 11

Honesty

Use honest scales and honest weights, an honest
ephah and an honest hin. I am the Lord your
God, who brought you out of Egypt.
—LEVITICUS 19:36 (NIV)

It's discouraging to think how many people are
shocked by honesty and how few by deceit.
—NOËL COWARD, BLITHE SPIRIT

Dear Lord, in all things, make us honest with ourselves,
with our loved ones, with our colleagues, and with
you. Pull us toward the truth like a moth to a flame.
And let us never waver in our honesty. Amen.

JANUARY 12

Righteous

This is the account of Noah and his family. Noah
was a righteous man, blameless among the people of
his time, and he walked faithfully with God.

—GENESIS 6:9 (NIV)

Until mankind can extend the circle of his compassion to
include all living things, he will never, himself, know peace.

—ALBERT SCHWEITZER, THEOLOGIAN
AND 1950 NOBEL PRIZE RECIPIENT

Dear God, we are ready for the fight—a righteous one.
Prepare us for battle; steel us for the task. Amen.

JANUARY 13

Gratitude

Let the message of Christ dwell among you richly as
you teach and admonish one another with all wisdom
through psalms, hymns, and songs from the Spirit,
singing to God with gratitude in your hearts.

—COLOSSIANS 3:16 (NIV)

Just don't give up trying to do what you really want to do. Where
there is love and inspiration, I don't think you can go wrong.

—ELLA FITZGERALD

Dear God, with eager expectation, we trust in your
power to bless us. And we will receive these blessings
with humility and gratitude today. Amen.

JANUARY 14

Disobedience

For just as through the disobedience of the one man the
many were made sinners, so also through the obedience
of the one man the many will be made righteous.

—ROMANS 5:19 (NIV)

What we think,
or what we know,
or what we believe,
is, in the end, of little consequence.
The only consequence is what we do.

—JOHN RUSKIN

Dear God, let us look past the opportunity for
disobedience and ever toward your light. Bless us, our
families, and our friends on this day. Amen.

JANUARY 15

Wealth

Wealth and honor come from you; you are the
ruler of all things. In your hands are strength and
power to exalt and give strength to all.
—1 CHRONICLES 29:12 (NIV)

Do what you can, with what you have, where you are.
—THEODORE ROOSEVELT

Dear God, it is you we want to impress. We don't want to boast
of wealth or power but of pleasing you with our lives. Thank you
for this day. Please protect us from all harm and danger. Amen.

JANUARY 16

Eternal

Now this is eternal life: that they know you, the only
true God, and Jesus Christ, whom you have sent.

—JOHN 17:3 (NIV)

We don't have to engage in grand, heroic actions to
participate in the process of change.
Small acts, when multiplied by millions of people,
can transform the world.

—HOWARD ZINN, HISTORIAN

Dear God, remind us that our momentary struggles are just
that—momentary. Fix our eyes on what is eternal. Thank
you for being our bridge over troubled waters. Amen.

Restore

Then the Lord your God will restore your fortunes
and have compassion on you and gather you again
from all the nations where he scattered you.
—DEUTERONOMY 30:3 (NIV)

One of the things I learned the hard way was that it
doesn't pay to get discouraged. Keeping busy and making
optimism a way of life can restore your faith in yourself.
—LUCILLE BALL

Thank you, dear God, that this life is never over and your work
is never done. We will rejuvenate and get ready for the road
ahead. Please continue to keep your mighty hands on us. Amen.

Distractions

I am saying this for your own good, not to restrict you, but that
you may live in a right way in undivided devotion to the Lord.

—1 CORINTHIANS 7:35 (NIV)

I am only one, but still I am one.
I cannot do everything, but still I can do something;
And because I cannot do everything
I will not refuse to do the something that I can do.

—HELEN KELLER

Dear God, let us resist not your Spirit. When we hear your voice,
let us move—even when it's tough. Open our ears today. Increase
our flexibility. Remove distractions that would drown you out. Let
us resist not your Sprit. And when you speak, let us move. Amen.

JANUARY 19

Unafraid

❦

He guided them safely, so they were unafraid;
but the sea engulfed their enemies.
—PSALM 78:53 (NIV)

A man who stands for nothing will fall for anything!
— MALCOLM X

Dear God, if this is our time to do a new thing, give
us the courage to act boldly, unafraid. Amen.

JANUARY 20

Obedience

Walk in obedience to all that the Lord your God has
commanded you, so that you may live and prosper and
prolong your days in the land that you will possess.
—DEUTERONOMY 5:23 (NIV)

People who are willing to give up freedom for the sake of
short-term security deserve neither freedom nor security.
— BENJAMIN FRANKLIN (1706–1790)

Dear God, we know you have some surprises up
your sleeve. We will walk this road of obedience
and let you do your work in us. Amen.

Faith in Action

Now faith is confidence in what we hope for
and assurance about what we do not see.

—HEBREWS 11:1 (NIV)

I believe in Christianity as I believe that the sun has risen: not
only because I see it, but because by it I see everything else.

— C. S. LEWIS

Dear God, help us move from spiritual childhood to adulthood.
Connect us with the people and resources to grow in our faith
so that we can move from manna to sustainable food. Amen.

Temptation

No temptation has overtaken you except what is common to mankind. And God is faithful; he will not let you be tempted beyond what you can bear. But when you are tempted, he will also provide a way out so that you can endure it.

—1 CORINTHIANS 10:13 (NIV)

Laws and principles are not for the times when there is no temptation: they are for such moments as this, when body and soul rise in mutiny against their rigour ... If at my convenience I might break them, what would be their worth?"

— CHARLOTTE BRONTË, JANE EYRE

Dear God, thank you for giving us another day. We pray for your help with temptation on this day. Amen.

JANUARY 23

Pleasant

The boundary lines have fallen for me in pleasant places;
surely I have a delightful inheritance. —Psalm 16:6 (NIV)
Believe in yourself! Have faith in your abilities!
Without a humble but reasonable confidence in your
own powers, you cannot be successful or happy.

—VINCENT PEALE

Dear Lord, make our words pleasant. Let them
not just instruct or reprove—but bring sweetness
and health to all we encounter today. Amen.

Blessings

Surely you have granted him unending blessings and
made him glad with the joy of your presence.
—PSALM 21:6 (NIV)

Instead of getting angry at somebody for opposing you
on something, you're just praying for them. You just
pray blessings on them, blessings on their family.
—SAM BROWNBACK

Dear God, thank you for the new morning and the promise it
brings. Invigorate us today, so we can know its blessings. Amen.

JANUARY 25

Careful

Be careful that you do not forget the Lord your
God, failing to observe his commands, his laws and
his decrees that I am giving you this day.
—DEUTERONOMY 8:11 (NIV)

We have to be careful in how we use this light shined on us.
—MELINDA GATES

Dear God, we thank you for this day. We pray that
you will help us walk carefully now so that others can
walk confidently in our footsteps later. Amen.

JANUARY 26

Praise

Praise the Lord. Praise God in his sanctuary; praise him
in his mighty heavens. Praise him for his acts of power;
praise him for his surpassing greatness. Praise him with the
sounding of the trumpet, praise him with the harp and lyre.

—PSALM 150:1–3 (NIV)

I have to give all praise to the Man above, because I
never gave up on Him, and He never gave up on me.

—CHAD KELLY

Dear God, let us never grow so hungry for power that it
becomes the thing we praise. Let power come and power
go—while our minds are forever fixed on you. Amen.

JANUARY 27

Unexpected

Moreover, no one knows when their hour will come: As fish are
caught in a cruel net, or birds are taken in a snare, so people
are trapped by evil times that fall unexpectedly upon them.

—ECCLESIASTES 9:12 (NIV)

Nothing is more memorable than a smell. One scent can
be unexpected, momentary, and fleeting, yet conjure up
a childhood summer beside a lake in the mountains.

—DIANE ACKERMAN

Dear God, thank you for the unexpected. Our eyes are
open to see bright lights in new spaces. Amen.

Dishonesty

The Lord detests dishonest scales, but accurate weights find favor
with him. When pride comes, then comes disgrace, but with
humility comes wisdom. The integrity of the upright guides
them, but the unfaithful are destroyed by their duplicity.

—PROVERBS 11:1–3 (NIV)

Sin is more than turning our backs on God—
it is turning our backs on life! Immorality is much
more than adultery and dishonesty: it is living drab,
colorless, dreary, stale, unimaginative lives.

—MIKE YACONELLI

Dear Lord, in all things, make us honest. With ourselves.
With our loved ones. With our colleagues. With
you. Pull us toward the truth like a moth to a flame.
And let us never waver in our honesty. Amen.

JANUARY 29

Prepared

It must be prepared with oil on a griddle; bring it
well-mixed and present the grain offering broken
in pieces as an aroma pleasing to the Lord.

—LEVITICUS 6:21 (NIV)

All I do, really, is go to work and try to be
professional, be on time, and be prepared.

—BEN AFFLECK

Dear God, we thank you for this day. We are
ready for the fight, a righteous one. Please prepare
us for battle; steel us for the task. Amen.

JANUARY 30

Expectation

And they exceeded our expectations: They gave themselves first of all to the Lord, and then by the will of God also to us.

—2 CORINTHIANS 8:5 (NIV)

You can't base your life on other people's expectations.

—STEVIE WONDER

Dear God, thank you for another day. We pray with eager expectation, and we trust in your power to bless us. And will receive these blessings with humility and gratitude today. Amen.

JANUARY 31

Opportunity

Therefore, as we have opportunity, let us do good to all people, especially to those who belong to the family of believers.

—GALATIANS 6:10

You can't knock on opportunity's door and not be ready.

—BRUNO MARS

Dear God, thank you for another wake-up call. Please allow us look past the opportunity for disobedience and ever toward your light. Bless us, our families, and our friends on this day. Amen.

FEBRUARY 1

Stumble

We all stumble in many ways. Anyone who is never at fault in
what they say is perfect, able to keep their whole body in check.
—JAMES 3:2 (NIV)

Keep on going and the chances are you will stumble on
something, perhaps when you are least expecting it. I have
never heard of anyone stumbling on something sitting down.
—CHARLES KETTERING

Gracious Father, thank you for another day. We all fall
short and make mistakes in life from time to time, but we
thank you for giving us new mercies each day. Amen.

FEBRUARY 2

Nourishment

This will bring health to your body and
nourishment to your bones.

—PROVERBS 3:8 (NIV)

Food brings people together on many different levels. It's
nourishment of the soul and body; it's truly love.

—GIADA DE LAURENTIIS

Father, we thank you for this day. We pray for
discipline to make healthy choices today, to properly
nourish our bodies, minds, and spirits. Amen.

FEBRUARY 3

Productive

Again, it will be like a man going on a journey, who called
his servants and entrusted his wealth to them. To one he gave
five bags of gold, to another two bags, and to another one bag,
each according to his ability. Then he went on his journey.

—MATTHEW 25:14–15 (NIV)

If your focus in life is on being productive, when
things are not happening … one has to ask oneself,
"Is this worth a grown man's time?"

—BOB CORKER

Dear Father, we thank you for this day. We pray
to be courageous, disciplined, productive, and
compassionate—with a positive attitude. Amen.

FEBRUARY 4

Almighty

Because of your father's God, who helps you, because
of the Almighty, who blesses you with blessings
of the skies above, blessings of the deep springs
below, blessings of the breast and womb.
—GENESIS 49:25 (NIV)

The civil rights movement was based on faith. Many of us
who were participants in this movement saw our involvement
as an extension of our faith. We saw ourselves doing the work
of the Almighty. Segregation and racial discrimination were
not in keeping with our faith, so we had to do something.
—JOHN LEWIS

Father, thank you for this day. We pray to never take your
many blessings for granted. Thank you for all things. Amen.

FEBRUARY 5

Breakthrough

Ask and it will be given to you; seek and you will find;
knock and the door will be opened to you. For everyone
who asks receives; the one who seeks finds; and to
the one who knocks, the door will be opened.

—MATTHEW 7:7–8 (NIV)

Instead of me having a breakdown, I'm focusing
on me having a breakthrough.

—TERRELL OWENS

Thank you, Father, for this day. We pray for
increases, financial breakthroughs, and business
promotions. Bless us in a mighty way. Amen.

FEBRUARY 6

Adore

Take me away with you—let us hurry! Let the king bring me
into his chambers. We rejoice and delight in you; we will praise
your love more than wine. How right they are to adore you!

—SONG OF SONGS 1:4 (NIV)

Everybody can adore you because you're on
television, but at the end of the day, when you're no
longer on TV, who's still there? It's family.

—ROLAND MARTIN

Dear God, thank you for all things big or small. We pray to be
our very best on this day with your help. We adore you. Amen.

FEBRUARY 7

Granted

The Lord was with him; he showed him kindness and
granted him favor in the eyes of the prison warden.
—GENESIS 39:21 (NIV)

It's human nature to start taking things for granted
again when danger isn't banging loudly on the door.
—DAVID HACKWORTH

Father, thank you for this day and the basic things of life, which
we often take for granted, like shelter, food, and jobs. Amen.

FEBRUARY 8

Judgmental

Do not judge, and you will not be judged. Do not condemn, and
you will not be condemned. Forgive, and you will be forgiven.
—LUKE 6:37 (NIV)

You can never get all the facts from just one newspaper,
and unless you have all the facts, you cannot make
proper judgements about what is going on.
—HARRY S. TRUMAN

Thank you, Father, for this day. You created each of us to be
different. We pray not to be judgmental of others. Amen.

FEBRUARY 9

Productive

Again, it will be like a man going on a journey, who called his servants and entrusted his wealth to them. To one he gave five bags of gold, to another two bags, and to another one bag, each according to his ability. Then he went on his journey. The man who had received five bags of gold went at once and put his money to work and gained five bags more.

—MATTHEW 25:14–30 (NIV)

Self-control, openness, the ability to engage with others, to plan and to persist—these are the attributes that get people in the door and on the job, and lead to productive lives.

—JAMES HECKMAN

Father, we thank you for this day. We pray to be alert and productive. Keep us safe from all harm and danger. Amen.

FEBRUARY 10

Stronger

But when someone stronger attacks and overpowers
him, he takes away the armor in which the man
trusted and divides up his plunder.

—LUKE 11:22 (NIV)

I have based my life on being strong enough to do anything.

—MONTEL WILLIAMS

Father, we thank you for this day. We pray to be stronger and
wiser than yesterday. Help us be focused and productive. Amen.

Wiser

Your commands are always with me and
make me wiser than my enemies.

—PSALM 119:98 (NIV)

Each generation imagines itself to be more intelligent than the one
that went before it, and wiser than the one that comes after it.

—GEORGE ORWELL

Dear Father, we thank you for this day. We pray to be stronger and
wiser than yesterday. Help us be focused and productive. Amen.

Mercy

And the Lord said, "I will cause all my goodness to pass in front of you, and I will proclaim my name, the Lord, in your presence. I will have mercy on whom I will have mercy, and I will have compassion on whom I will have compassion."

—EXODUS 33:19 (NIV)

There is no austerity equal to a balanced mind, and there is no happiness equal to contentment; there is no disease like covetousness, and no virtue like mercy.

—CHANAKYA

Dear God, thank you for waking us up this morning. We pray for your continuous grace, mercy, and tender loving care. Amen.

God's Will

But I will establish my covenant with you, and
you will enter the ark—you and your sons and
your wife and your sons' wives with you.

—GENESIS 6:18 (NIV)

If you have other gods before the Lord, your heart will be
turned away from serving the only true and living God, who
requires the whole heart, the undivided affections. All the
heart, all the soul, all the mind, and all the strength, does
God require. He will accept of nothing short of this.

—ELLEN G. WHITE

Father, we thank you for putting expiration dates
on people, places, and things in our lives. We
pray to follow your will for us. Amen.

FEBRUARY 14

Gratitude

Let the message of Christ dwell among you richly as
you teach and admonish one another with all wisdom
through psalms, hymns, and songs from the Spirit,
singing to God with gratitude in your hearts.
—COLOSSIANS 3:16 (NIV)

Gratitude makes sense of our past, brings peace
for today, and creates a vision for tomorrow.
—MELODY BEATTIE

Father, we thank you for this day. We pray for an attitude of
gratitude. We appreciate all that you have done for us. Amen.

FEBRUARY 15

Distractions

But Martha was distracted by all the preparations that had to be made. She came to him and asked, "Lord, don't you care that my sister has left me to do the work by myself? Tell her to help me!"

—LUKE 10:40 (NIV)

Successful people maintain a positive focus in life no matter what is going on around them. They stay focused on their past successes rather than their past failures, and on the next action steps they need to take to get them closer to the fulfillment of their goals rather than all the other distractions that life presents to them.

—JACK CANFIELD

Father, thank you for strong and creative minds.
We pray for the removal of distractions that keep us
from your primary purpose in our lives. Amen.

FEBRUARY 16

Spiritual Gifts

Now about the gifts of the Spirit, brothers and sisters, I do not want you to be uninformed. You know that when you were pagans, somehow or other you were influenced and led astray to mute idols. Therefore I want you to know that no one who is speaking by the Spirit of God says, "Jesus be cursed," and no one can say, "Jesus is Lord," except by the Holy Spirit.

—1 CORINTHIANS 12:1–3 (NIV)

Throughout our lives, God's grace bestows temporal blessings and spiritual gifts that magnify our abilities and enrich our lives. His grace refines us. His grace helps us become our best selves.

—DIETER F. UCHTDORF

Thank you, Father, for our spiritual gifts.
We pray to use them wisely. Amen.

FEBRUARY 17

Elderly

Stand up in the presence of the aged, show respect for
the elderly and revere your God. I am the Lord.

—LEVITICUS 19:32 (NIV)

The elderly are all someone's flesh and blood and we
cannot just shut them in a cupboard and hand over the
responsibility for taking care of them to the state.

—SIMON CALLOW

Dear God, we thank you for this day. We pray
for the elderly and those who care for them.
Grant them strength and patience. Amen.

Smiles

The Lord bless you and keep you; the Lord make his
face shine on you and be gracious to you; the Lord
turn his face toward you and give you peace..
—NUMBERS 6:24–26 (NIV)

Let my soul smile through my heart and my heart smile
through my eyes, that I may scatter rich smiles in sad hearts.
—PARAMAHANSA YOGANANDA

Thank you, God, for your warm embrace. We
pray that our outsides will match our insides.
Our smiles will be contagious. Amen.

Mind-Sets

Therefore, with minds that are alert and fully sober,
set your hope on the grace to be brought to you
when Jesus Christ is revealed at his coming.

—1 PETER 1:13 (NIV)

We need to make sure we're all working together to
change mindsets, to change attitudes, and to fight
against the bad habits that we have as a society.

—JUSTIN TRUDEAU

Father, thank you for strong and creative minds. We pray for the
removal of distractions that keep us from your purpose. Amen.

FEBRUARY 20

Spiritual Gifts and Talents

Now about the gifts of the Spirit, brothers and sisters, I do not want you to be uninformed. You know that when you were pagans, somehow or other you were influenced and led astray to mute idols. Therefore I want you to know that no one who is speaking by the Spirit of God says, "Jesus be cursed," and no one can say, "Jesus is Lord," except by the Holy Spirit.

—1 CORINTHIANS 12:1–3 (NIV)

Satan will advocate that it is cool to doubt spiritual gifts and the teachings of true prophets.

—DIETER F. UCHTDORF

Thank you, Father, for our spiritual gifts and talents. We pray to use them wisely. Thanks for opening doors of opportunities. Amen.

FEBRUARY 21

Will

Then I will make my covenant between me and
you and will greatly increase your numbers.
—GENESIS 17:2

Failure will never overtake me if my determination
to succeed is strong enough.
—OG MANDINO

Dear Father, we thank you for another day. We are
praying to do your will and stay away from self-will on
this day. Please help us stay focused on you. Amen.

FEBRUARY 22

Obedient

So the Word of God spread. The number of disciples
in Jerusalem increased rapidly, and a large number
of priests became obedient to the faith.

—ACTS 6:7 (NIV)

My relationship with God has gotten so much stronger. He's
always had his hand on me. He always guided me. I didn't always
go where he wanted me to go. But He always had me. Now that
I'm actually listening and being obedient, life is so much better.

—DMX

Dear God, we thank you for your precious love. We pray to be
more obedient to your will for us. Surrendering all to you. Amen.

Minds

Fix these words of mine in your hearts and minds; tie them as symbols on your hands and bind them on your foreheads.
—DEUTERONOMY 11:18 (NIV)

No person, no place, and no thing has any power over us, for "we" are the only thinkers in our mind. When we create peace and harmony and balance in our minds, we will find it in our lives. —LOUISE L. HAY

Dear God, thank you for this week. We pray for good physical, mental, and spiritual health. Please guide us this day. Amen.

FEBRUARY 24

Smile

If I say, "I will forget my complaint, I will
change my expression, and smile."
—JOB 9:27 (NIV)

Let my soul smile through my heart and my heart smile
through my eyes, that I may scatter rich smiles in sad hearts.
— PARAMAHANSA YOGANANDA

Thank you, God, for your warm embrace. We pray
that our outsides will match our insides. That our
smiles will be contagious today. Amen.

FEBRUARY 25

Peace

And the peace of God, which transcends all understanding,
will guard your hearts and your minds in Christ Jesus.
—PHILIPPIANS 4:7 (NIV)

Gratitude makes sense of our past, brings peace
for today, and creates a vision for tomorrow.
—MELODY BEATTIE

Dear God, please grant us the serenity to accept the things we
cannot change and the wisdom to know the difference. Amen.

Protection

But let all who take refuge in you be glad; let them
ever sing for joy. Spread your protection over them that
those who love your name may rejoice in you.

—PSALM 5:11 (NIV)

I cannot think of any need in childhood as strong
as the need for a father's protection.

—SIGMUND FREUD

Dear God, we thank you for this day. We pray to stay focused
and productive. Please guide and protect us. Amen.

FEBRUARY 27

Children

People were also bringing babies to Jesus for him to place his hands on them. When the disciples saw this, they rebuked them. But Jesus called the children to him and said, "Let the little children come to me, and do not hinder them, for the kingdom of God belongs to such as these. Truly I tell you, anyone who will not receive the kingdom of God like a little child will never enter it." Luke 18:15–17 (NIV) When my children were growing up, we began every family meal—which included breakfast and dinner every day—with a prayer. We are Jewish and so it was the prayer over bread, when we were having bread, or the catch-all prayer for everything when we weren't.

—EZEKIEL EMANUEL

Thank you, God, for this day. We pray for our children and grandchildren. Bless them all from the youngest to the oldest. Amen.

Provision

Joseph gave orders to fill their bags with grain, to put each man's silver back in his sack, and to give them provisions for their journey. After this was done for them.

— GENESIS 42:25 (NIV)

Rejecting the fundamental provision of the Civil Rights Act is a rejection of the foundational promise of America that all men and women should be treated equally, a promise for which many Americans have lost their lives.

—JOHN YARMUTH

Dear God, thank you for provision. Sometimes we find ourselves in the valleys of life, but you always bring us through. Thank you. Amen.

MARCH 1

Wiser

Your commands are always with me and
make me wiser than my enemies.
—PSALM 119:98 (NIV)

Each generation imagines itself to be more intelligent than the one
that went before it, and wiser than the one that comes after it.
—GEORGE ORWELL

Father, we thank you for this day. We pray to be stronger and
wiser than yesterday. Help us be focused and productive. Amen.

MARCH 2

Grace

For it is by grace you have been saved, through
faith—and this is not from yourselves, it is the gift of
God— not by works, so that no one can boast.
—EPHESIANS 2:8–9 (NIV)

Happiness cannot be traveled to, owned, earned, worn,
or consumed. Happiness is the spiritual experience of
living every minute with love, grace, and gratitude.
—DENIS WAITLEY

Dear God, thank you for waking us up this morning. We pray
for your continuous grace, mercy, and tender loving care. Amen.

MARCH 3

God's Will

Paul, an apostle of Christ Jesus by the will
of God, and Timothy our brother,
To God's holy people in Colossae, the faithful
brothers and sisters in Christ:
Grace and peace to you from God our Father.

—COLOSSIANS 1:1–2 (NIV)

We live in a disposable, "cast-off and throw-away"
society that has largely lost any real sense of permanence.
Ours is a world of expiration dates, limited shelf life,
and planned obsolescence. Nothing is absolute.

—MYLES MUNROE

Father, we thank you for putting expiration dates
on people, places, and things in our lives. We
pray to follow your will for us. Amen.

MARCH 4

Gratitude

Let the message of Christ dwell among you richly as
you teach and admonish one another with all wisdom
through psalms, hymns, and songs from the Spirit,
singing to God with gratitude in your hearts.
—COLOSSIANS 3:16 (NIV)

Happiness cannot be traveled to, owned, earned, worn,
or consumed. Happiness is the spiritual experience of
living every minute with love, grace, and gratitude.
—DENIS WAITLEY

Father, we thank you for this day. We pray for an attitude of
gratitude. We appreciate all that you have done for us. Amen.

MARCH 5

Distractions

I am saying this for your own good, not to restrict you, but that
you may live in a right way in undivided devotion to the Lord.

—1 CORINTHIANS 7:35 (NIV)

Successful people maintain a positive focus in life no matter what
is going on around them. They stay focused on their past successes
rather than their past failures, and on the next action steps they
need to take to get them closer to the fulfillment of their goals
rather than all the other distractions that life presents to them.

—JACK CANFIELD

Father, thank you for strong and creative minds. We pray for the
removal of distractions that keep us from your purpose. Amen.

MARCH 6

Talents

The total amount of the gold from the wave offering
used for all the work on the sanctuary was 29 talents
and 730 shekels, according to the sanctuary shekel.

—EXODUS 38:24 (NIV)

I believe that God has put gifts and talents and ability on the
inside of every one of us. When you develop that and you believe
in yourself and you believe that you're a person of influence and a
person of purpose, I believe you can rise up out of any situation.

—JOEL OSTEEN

Thank you, Father, for our spiritual gifts and
talents. We pray to use them wisely. Thanks for
opening doors of opportunities. Amen.

MARCH 7

Strength

He gives strength to the weary and
increases the power of the weak.
—ISAIAH 40:29 (NIV)

Each one of us can do a good deed, every day and
everywhere. In hospitals in desperate need of volunteers,
in homes for the elderly where our parents and
grandparents are longing for a smile, a listening ear, in
the street, in our workplaces and especially at home.
—SHARI ARISON

Dear God, we thank you for this day. We pray
for the elderly and those who care for them—
grant them strength and patience. Amen.

MARCH 8

Surrender

If anyone does attack you, it will not be my doing;
whoever attacks you will surrender to you.
—ISAIAH 54:15 (NIV)

Control and surrender have to be kept in balance. That's what
surfers do—take control of the situation, then be carried, then
take control. In the last few thousand years, we've become
incredibly adept technically. We've treasured the controlling
part of ourselves and neglected the surrendering part.
—BRIAN ENO

Dear God, we thank you for your precious love. We pray to be
more obedient to your will for us. Surrendering all to you. Amen.

MARCH 9

Spiritual Health

I long to see you so that I may impart to you
some spiritual gift to make you strong.
—ROMANS 1:11 (NIV)

Spiritually good people, pure in heart, who long for the
Blessed Sacrament but cannot receive at the time, can
receive spiritually ... even a hundred times a day, in sickness
and in health, with immeasurable grace and profit.
—JOHANNES TAULER

Dear God, thank you for this week. We pray for good physical,
mental, and spiritual health. Please guide us this day. Amen.

MARCH 10

Contagious

The Lord said to Moses and Aaron, "When anyone has
a swelling or a rash or a shiny spot on their skin that
may be a defiling skin disease, they must be brought to
Aaron the priest or to one of his sons who is a priest."

—LEVITICUS 13:1 (NIV)

You may not always have a comfortable life and you will
not always be able to solve all of the world's problems at
once but don't ever underestimate the importance you
can have because history has shown us that courage can
be contagious and hope can take on a life of its own.

—MICHELLE OBAMA

Thank you, God, for your warm embrace. We
pray that our outsides will match our insides.
Our smiles will be contagious. Amen.

MARCH 11

Happiness

If a man has recently married, he must not be sent to war or have any other duty laid on him. For one year he is to be free to stay at home and bring happiness to the wife he has married.

—DEUTERONOMY 24:5 (NIV)

Happiness is not something you postpone for the future; it is something you design for the present.

—JIM ROHN

Dear God, thank you for this day. We pray for your peace, love, joy, and happiness. Illuminate your marvelous light in us. Amen.

MARCH 12

Wisdom

If any of you lacks wisdom, you should ask God, who gives
generously to all without finding fault, and it will be given to you.
—JAMES 1:5 (NIV)

God grant me the serenity to accept the things I
cannot change, the courage to change the things I
can, and the wisdom to know the difference.
—REINHOLD NIEBUHR

Dear God, please grant us the serenity to accept the things we
cannot change and the wisdom to know the difference. Help us
understand your will for our lives and be faithful to you. Amen.

MARCH 13

Opportunities

Therefore, as we have opportunity, let us do good to all people, especially to those who belong to the family of believers.

—GALATIANS 6:10 (NIV)

I can control my destiny, but not my fate. Destiny means there are opportunities to turn right or left, but fate is a one-way street. I believe we all have the choice as to whether we fulfil our destiny, but our fate is sealed.

—PAULO COELHO

Dear God, we are grateful for this day. We thank you for opening doors of opportunities for us. Amen.

MARCH 14

Productive

Again, it will be like a man going on a journey, who called his servants and entrusted his wealth to them. To one he gave five bags of gold, to another two bags, and to another one bag, each according to his ability. Then he went on his journey. The man who had received five bags of gold went at once and put his money to work and gained five bags more. So also, the one with two bags of gold gained two more. But the man who had received one bag went off, dug a hole in the ground and hid his master's money.

—MATTHEW 25:14–18 (NIV)

The bottom line is, when people are crystal clear about the most important priorities of the organization and team they work with and prioritized their work around those top priorities, not only are they many times more productive, they discover they have the time they need to have a whole life.

—STEPHEN COVEY

Dear God, we thank you for this day. We pray to stay focused and productive. Please guide and protect us. Amen.

MARCH 15

Guidance

For lack of guidance a nation falls, but victory
is won through many advisers.
—PROVERBS 11:14 (NIV)

Be true to yourself, help others, make each day your masterpiece,
make friendship a fine art, drink deeply from good books—
especially the Bible, build a shelter against a rainy day, give
thanks for your blessings and pray for guidance every day.
—JOHN WOODEN

Dear Father, we thank you for another day. We are praying for
guidance. Help us be better than we were yesterday. Amen.

MARCH 16

Provision

So the sons of Israel did this. Joseph gave them
carts, as Pharaoh had commanded, and he also
gave them provisions for their journey.
—GENESIS 45:21 (NIV)

And that's really what's happening in this country is a
violation of the First Commandment. We have become
a country entrenched in idolatry, and that idolatry is the
dependency upon our government. We're supposed to
depend upon God for our protection and our provision
and for our daily bread, not for our government.
—SHARRON ANGLE

Dear God, thank you for provision. Sometimes we find ourselves
in the valleys of life, but you always bring us through. Amen.

MARCH 17

Homeless

To this very hour we go hungry and thirsty, we are in
rags, we are brutally treated, we are homeless.
—1 CORINTHIANS 4:11 (NIV)

People can be so apathetic. They continue to ignore the real people
trapped in poverty and homelessness. It's almost maddening.
—DAPHNE ZUNIGA

Dear God, we thank you for the power of your
Word and prayer. Bless the homeless, the sick, active
military, veterans, and the jobless. Amen.

Knowledge

The heart of the discerning acquires knowledge,
for the ears of the wise seek it out.
—PROVERBS 18:15 (NIV)

For beautiful eyes, look for the good in others; for
beautiful lips, speak only words of kindness; and for poise,
walk with the knowledge that you are never alone.
—AUDREY HEPBURN

Dear God, we thank you for another week. We
pray for your strength, wisdom, knowledge, and
understanding. We love you. Amen.

MARCH 19

Humbly

Then the king said to Ziba, "All that belonged to
Mephibosheth is now yours." "I humbly bow," Ziba said.
"May I find favor in your eyes, my lord the king."
—2 SAMUEL 16:4 (NIV)

Prayer is a privilege and the soul's sincere desire. We can move
beyond routine and "checklist" prayers and engage in meaningful
prayer as we appropriately ask in faith and act, as we patiently
persevere through the trial of our faith, and as we humbly
acknowledge and accept "not my will, but Thine, be done."
—DAVID A. BEDNAR

Dear God, we are thankful for all you have done
for us down through the years. We humbly ask
you, "What can we do for you?" Amen.

Grateful

But I, with shouts of grateful praise, will sacrifice
to you. What I have vowed I will make good. I
will say, "Salvation comes from the Lord."
—JONAH 2:9 (NIV)

I believe if you keep your faith, you keep your trust, you keep the
right attitude, if you're grateful, you'll see God open up new doors.
—JOEL OSTEEN

Dear God, we thank you for this day. We pray to be grateful for
life, family, friends, shelter, jobs, food, and good health. Amen.

MARCH 21

Positive

Finally, brothers and sisters, whatever is true, whatever
is noble, whatever is right, whatever is pure, whatever is
lovely, whatever is admirable—if anything is excellent
or praiseworthy—think about such things.

—PHILIPPIANS 4:8 (NIV)

A positive attitude causes a chain reaction of
positive thoughts, events, and outcomes. It is a
catalyst and it sparks extraordinary results.

—WADE BOGGS

Dear God, we thank you for this day. We pray to stay positive
and not give life to negativity. Bless us on this day. Amen.

MARCH 22

Creation

Let all creation rejoice before the Lord, for he comes,
he comes to judge the earth. He will judge the world in
righteousness and the peoples in his faithfulness.

—PSALM 96:13 (NIV)

God wants us to know that life is a series of beginnings,
not endings. Just as graduations are not terminations,
but commencements. Creation is an ongoing process,
and when we create a perfect world where love and
compassion are shared by all, suffering will cease.

—BERNIE SIEGEL

Dear God, we thank you for your creation. We pray to live this
day to its fullest for you only give us one day at a time. Amen.

MARCH 23

Progressive

The king should know that we went to the district of
Judah, to the temple of the great God. The people are
building it with large stones and placing the timbers in
the walls. The work is being carried on with diligence
and is making rapid progress under their direction.

—EZRA 5:8 (NIV)

We all want progress, but if you're on the wrong road, progress
means doing an about-turn and walking back to the right road; in
that case, the man who turns back soonest is the most progressive.

—C. S. LEWIS

Dear God, thank you for this day. We pray to be progressive and
not regressive. Give us clean hearts and strong minds. Amen.

Gift

Then to the place the Lord your God will choose as a dwelling for his Name—there you are to bring everything I command you: your burnt offerings and sacrifices, your tithes and special gifts, and all the choice possessions you have vowed to the Lord.

—DEUTERONOMY 12:11 (NIV)

Your talent is God's gift to you. What you
do with it is your gift back to God.

—LEO BUSCAGLIA

Dear God, thank you for this gift of life. We pray to utilize this precious gift to its fullest, sharing love and peace. Amen.

MARCH 25

Endure

As long as the earth endures, seedtime and harvest, cold and
heat, summer and winter, day and night will never cease.

—GENESIS 8:22 (NIV)

A hero is an ordinary individual who finds the strength to
persevere and endure in spite of overwhelming obstacles.

—CHRISTOPHER REEVE

Dear God, we glorify you. Give us the strength
to endure the challenges of life—so that we
may continue to push forward. Amen.

MARCH 26

Trust

Trust in the Lord with all your heart and lean not
on your own understanding; in all your ways submit
to him, and he will make your paths straight.
—PROVERBS 3:5–6 (NIV)

I truly believe that everything that we do and everyone that we
meet is put in our path for a purpose. There are no accidents;
we're all teachers—if we're willing to pay attention to the lessons
we learn, trust our positive instincts and not be afraid to take
risks or wait for some miracle to come knocking at our door.
—MARLA GIBBS

Dear God, bless us on this day. We pray to trust you in and out
of seasons when things are good or bad, up or down. Amen.

MARCH 27

Deliverance

But God sent me ahead of you to preserve for you a remnant
on earth and to save your lives by a great deliverance.
—GENESIS 45:7 (NIV)

The work of healing is not my work, but by faith, healing
is done. The work of deliverance, great and mighty
deliverance, is not my work but is my faith in Him. It is
not the works of righteousness which I have done, but
according to His grace. I am a product of His grace.
—T. B. JOSHUA

Dear God, thank you for our wake-up call. We pray for
increase, breakthroughs, and deliverance on this day. Amen.

MARCH 28

Guidance

Saul died because he was unfaithful to the Lord; he did not keep
the Word of the Lord and even consulted a medium for guidance.

—1 CHRONICLES 10:13 (NIV)

A man has to learn that he cannot command things, but
that he can command himself; that he cannot coerce
the wills of others, but that he can mold and master his
own will: and things serve him who serves Truth; people
seek guidance of him who is master of himself.

—JAMES ALLEN

Dear God, we thank you for another week. We pray for your
guidance and that we keep an attitude of gratitude. Amen.

MARCH 29

Forgiveness

Peter replied, "Repent and be baptized, every one of you,
in the name of Jesus Christ for the forgiveness of your
sins. And you will receive the gift of the Holy Spirit."
—ACTS 2:38 (NIV)

The weak can never forgive. Forgiveness
is the attribute of the strong.
—MAHATMA GANDHI

Dear God, we thank you for your forgiveness. We pray that we
can forgive others and move on without resentments. Amen.

MARCH 30

Praise

David said to Abigail, "Praise be to the Lord, the God
of Israel, who has sent you today to meet me."
—1 SAMUEL 25:32 (NIV)

The more you praise and celebrate your life,
the more there is in life to celebrate.
—OPRAH WINFREY

Dear God, we praise you for this day. Help us stay strong
and walk in faith. Guide us through this day. Amen.

MARCH 31

Peace

Do not suppose that I have come to bring peace to the earth.
I did not come to bring peace, but a sword. For I have come
to turn "a man against his father, a daughter against her
mother, a daughter-in-law against her mother-in-law—a
man's enemies will be the members of his own household."

—MATTHEW 10:34–36 (NIV)

Peace is the beauty of life. It is sunshine. It is the smile
of a child, the love of a mother, the joy of a father, the
togetherness of a family. It is the advancement of man,
the victory of a just cause, the triumph of truth.

—MENACHEM BEGIN

Dear God, we thank you once again for this day. We are praying
for peace, love, wisdom, and understanding. Keep us safe. Amen.

APRIL 1

Enemies

Whenever the ark set out, Moses said, "Rise up, Lord! May
your enemies be scattered; may your foes flee before you."
—NUMBERS 10:35 (NIV)

Jealousy is no more than feeling alone against smiling enemies.
—ELIZABETH BOWEN

Father, with your help we come against the enemies
within us: insecurity, self-centeredness, pride,
jealousy, fear, anger, and envy. Amen.

APRIL 2

Productive

Again, it will be like a man going on a journey, who called his servants and entrusted his wealth to them. To one he gave five bags of gold, to another two bags, and to another one bag, each according to his ability. Then he went on his journey. The man who had received five bags of gold went at once and put his money to work and gained five bags more.

—MATTHEW 25:14–30 (NIV)

As long as your intentions are solid and about growth and progression and being productive and not being idle, then you're doing good in my book.

—FRANK OCEAN

Dear Father God, thank you for this day. We are praying to be productive, not waste precious time on things that don't matter, and focus on the things that do. Amen.

APRIL 3

Presence

You make known to me the path of life; you will fill me with
joy in your presence, with eternal pleasures at your right hand.
—PSALM 16:11 (NIV)

Appreciation is the highest form of prayer, for it
acknowledges the presence of good wherever you
shine the light of your thankful thoughts.
—ALAN COHEN

Dear Father, we pray to keep our presence in the moments
of this day, to be grateful for all your many blessings. Thank
you for sharing your precious love with us. Amen.

APRIL 4

Debts

And forgive us our debts, as we also have forgiven our debtors.
—MATTHEW 6:12 (NIV)

We tend to focus on assets and forget about debts. Financial security requires facing up to the big picture: assets minus debts.
—SUZE ORMAN

Dear Father, thank you for the wake-up call. Give us this day our daily bread. Forgive us our debts as we forgive our debtors. Amen.

APRIL 5

Understanding

And the peace of God, which transcends all understanding,
will guard your hearts and your minds in Christ Jesus.

—PHILIPPIANS 4:7 (NIV)

We need to reject any politics that targets people because of
race or religion. This isn't a matter of political correctness.
It's a matter of understanding what makes us strong. The
world respects us not just for our arsenal; it respects us for our
diversity and our openness and the way we respect every faith.

—BARACK OBAMA

Father, thank you for this day. We are praying for your
peace and understanding. We will walk in faith and
let go of all fear. Direct our footsteps. Amen.

APRIL 6

Spiritual Growth

For this reason I kneel before the Father, from whom
every family in heaven and on earth derives its name. I
pray that out of his glorious riches he may strengthen you
with power through his Spirit in your inner being.
—EPHESIANS 3:14–21 (NIV)

A spiritual partnership is a partnership between equals
for the purpose of spiritual growth. Spiritual partners use
their delightful experiences together as well as their power
struggles to learn about themselves and change themselves.
—GARY ZUKAV

Father, we thank you for our spiritual growth. As
we get older, we grow closer to you. As we work
out spiritually, you work with us. Amen.

APRIL 7

Promises

For no matter how many promises God has made,
they are "Yes" in Christ. And so through him the
"Amen" is spoken by us to the glory of God.
—2 CORINTHIANS 1:20 (NIV)

Life is too short to worry about anything. You had better
enjoy it because the next day promises nothing.
—ERIC DAVIS

Almighty Father who has all power in heaven and
earth, thank you for your precious love and promises of
abundance. We stand on your Word today. Amen.

APRIL 8

Renewing

Do not conform to the pattern of this world, but be transformed by the renewing of your mind. Then you will be able to test and approve what God's will is—his good, pleasing, and perfect will.

—ROMANS 12:2 (NIV)

Enthusiasm is followed by disappointment and even depression, and then by renewed enthusiasm.

—MURRAY GELL-MANN

Almighty Father, we thank you for your creation. We are praying for a renewing of our minds so that we can understand your primary purpose for us. Amen.

APRIL 9

Obey

Children, obey your parents in the Lord, for this is right.
"Honor your father and mother"—which is the first
commandment with a promise— "so that it may go well
with you and that you may enjoy long life on the earth."
—EPHESIANS 6:1 (NIV)

The Bible tells us that God will meet all our needs. He feeds
the birds of the air and clothes the grass with the splendor
of lilies. How much more, then, will He care for us, who
are made in His image? Our only concern is to obey the
heavenly Father and leave the consequences to Him.

— CHARLES STANLEY

Almighty Father, we glorify you on this day. Give us the desire
to obey you and the power to do what pleases you. Amen.

APRIL 10

Connection

They have lost connection with the head, from whom
the whole body, supported and held together by its
ligaments and sinews, grows as God causes it to grow.
—COLOSSIANS 2:19 (NIV)

In my deepest, darkest moments, what really got me through was
a prayer. Sometimes my prayer was 'Help me.' Sometimes a prayer
was 'Thank you.' What I've discovered is that intimate connection
and communication with my creator will always get me through
because I know my support, my help, is just a prayer away.
—IYANLA VANZANT

Father, we thank you for this great connection with you.
Thank you for a life of abundance. We walk in faith,
love, and security because of your love for us. Amen.

APRIL 11

Renewal

If someone dies, will they live again? All the days of my
hard service I will wait for my renewal to come.
—JOB 14:14 (NIV)

We don't even know how strong we are until we are
forced to bring that hidden strength forward. In times of
tragedy, of war, of necessity, people do amazing things. The
human capacity for survival and renewal is awesome.
—ISABEL ALLENDE

Almighty Father, thank you for this day. We are praying
for renewal of our minds. Teach us things that will help
us grow spiritually. Increase our faith in you. Amen.

APRIL 12

Positivity

Finally, brothers and sisters, whatever is true, whatever
is noble, whatever is right, whatever is pure, whatever is
lovely, whatever is admirable—if anything is excellent
or praiseworthy—think about such things.

—PHILIPPIANS 4:8 (NIV)

Surround yourself with good people; surround
yourself with positivity and people who are going
to challenge you to make you better.

—ALI KRIEGER

Father, we are grateful for this day. Thank you for the
power of the tongue. We speak positivity into our lives for
healing, finances, families, and relationships. Amen.

APRIL 13

Forgiveness

This is my blood of the covenant, which is poured
out for many for the forgiveness of sins.
—MATTHEW 26:28 (NIV)

There is no love without forgiveness, and
there is no forgiveness without love.
—BRYANT H. MCGILL

Father, thank you for this day. Please help us with patience
and humility. Show us how to forgive as we ask for
forgiveness. We let go and let you have your way. Amen.

APRIL 14

Stewards

Each of you should use whatever gift you have received to serve
others, as faithful stewards of God's grace in its various forms.
—1 PETER 4:10 (NIV)

Our best and brightest must conceive of themselves
as stewards of our society and confront the critical
challenges of our time. It's the best bet for our society, for
entrepreneurs, and for the investors who believe in them.
—JOE LONSDALE

Father, thank you for this day's many gifts. We are grateful
for all of your many blessings through the years. We are
praying to be good stewards of your gifts. Amen.

APRIL 15

Grace

For it is by grace you have been saved, through
faith—and this is not from yourselves, it is the gift of
God— not by works, so that no one can boast.
—EPHESIANS 2:8–9 (NIV)

Happiness cannot be traveled to, owned, earned, worn,
or consumed. Happiness is the spiritual experience of
living every minute with love, grace, and gratitude.
—DENIS WAITLEY

Thank you, Father, for your grace. We are praying for
self-discipline and the power to rise above any situations
that are keeping us from moving forward. Amen.

APRIL 16

Gentle

A gentle answer turns away wrath, but a harsh word stirs up anger. The tongue of the wise adorns knowledge, but the mouth of the fool gushes folly. The eyes of the Lord are everywhere, keeping watch on the wicked and the good.

—PROVERBS 15:1 (NIV)

A gentle word, a kind look, a good-natured smile can work wonders and accomplish miracles.

—WILLIAM HAZLITT

Father God, we thank you for this day. We pray to stay centered with you, allowing you to direct us. We want to hear your gentle voice over the noise of this world. Amen.

APRIL 17

Wholeness

For to us a child is born, to us a son is given, and the government will be on his shoulders. And he will be called Wonderful Counselor, Mighty God, Everlasting Father, Prince of Peace.

—ISAIAH 9:6 (NIV)

My prayer became "May I find peace ... May I love this life no matter what." I was seeking an inner refuge, an experience of presence and wholeness that could carry me through whatever losses might come.

—TARA BRACH

Father, thank you for this day. We pray for wholeness. We come against brokenness: broken marriages, relationships, hearts, minds, and spirits. Amen.

APRIL 18

Focused

Let your eyes look straight ahead; fix your gaze directly before you.
—PROVERBS 4:25 (NIV)

Successful people maintain a positive focus in life no matter what is going on around them. They stay focused on their past successes rather than their past failures, and on the next action steps they need to take to get them closer to the fulfillment of their goals rather than all the other distractions that life presents to them.
—JACK CANFIELD

Father, we thank you for this day, we are grateful for another week. We pray to stay focused, productive, and progressive. Thank you for new mercies. Amen.

Traps

Then you may be sure that the Lord your God will no
longer drive out these nations before you. Instead, they
will become snares and traps for you, whips on your
backs and thorns in your eyes, until you perish from this
good land, which the Lord your God has given you.

—JOSHUA 23:13 (NIV)

Kindness and intelligence don't always deliver us from the pitfalls
and traps: there are always failures of love, of will, of imagination.
There is no way to take the danger out of human relationships.

—BARBARA GRIZZUTI HARRISON

Father, we thank you for this day. Help us stay focused
and consult you before making any major decisions. We
pray not to fall into traps set to hinder us. Amen.

APRIL 20

Shelter

Whoever dwells in the shelter of the Most High will rest in the shadow of the Almighty. I will say of the Lord, "He is my refuge and my fortress, my God, in whom I trust." Surely he will save you from the fowler's snare and from the deadly pestilence.

—PSALM 91:1 (NIV)

Be true to yourself, help others, make each day your masterpiece, make friendship a fine art, drink deeply from good books— especially the Bible, build a shelter against a rainy day, give thanks for your blessings and pray for guidance every day.

—JOHN WOODEN

Father, we are praying for our children on this day. Please allow them to have full, healthy lives without abuse, fear, or lack. Shelter them from all danger. Amen.

APRIL 21

Footsteps

Direct my footsteps according to your
word; let no sin rule over me.
—PSALM 119:133 (NIV)

I've always had a passion for giving back. It's a family
tradition that comes from my devout parents. They were
always giving back and serving the community. So when
I became fortunate enough and blessed to play the game
of basketball, I was also fortunate enough to follow in my
parents' footsteps and give back like the way they did.
—DIKEMBE MUTOMBO

Thank you, Father, for another wake-up call. We are praying
not to be anxious or get ahead of you. Order our footsteps
in the directions you desire. We have faith in you. Amen.

Confidence

So do not throw away your confidence; it will be richly rewarded.
—HEBREWS 10:35 (NIV)

Love is friendship that has caught fire. It is quiet
understanding, mutual confidence, sharing and forgiving. It
is loyalty through good and bad times. It settles for less than
perfection and makes allowances for human weaknesses.
—ANN LANDERS

Dear gracious Father, we thank you for this day. Please
prepare us to face this day with confidence and assurance
that we can master this day with your help. Amen.

APRIL 23

Transportation

As they approached Jerusalem and came to Bethphage
and Bethany at the Mount of Olives, Jesus sent two of
his disciples, saying to them, "Go to the village ahead
of you, and just as you enter it, you will find a colt tied
there, which no one has ever ridden. Untie it and bring it
here. If anyone asks you, 'Why are you doing this?' say,
'The Lord needs it and will send it back here shortly.'"

—MARK 11:1–3 (NIV)

Among all the marvels of modern invention, that with
which I am most concerned is, of course, air transportation.
Flying is perhaps the most dramatic of recent scientific
attainment. In the brief span of thirty-odd years, the world
has seen an inventor's dream first materialized by the Wright
brothers at Kitty Hawk become an everyday actuality.

—AMELIA EARHART

Father, we thank you for providing us with our basic
needs: shelter, food, clothes, jobs, good health, and
transportation. Please continue to bless us. Amen.

APRIL 24

Loneliness

So do not fear, for I am with you; do not be dismayed,
for I am your God. I will strengthen you and help you;
I will uphold you with my righteous right hand.

—ISAIAH 41:10 (NIV)

Our uniqueness makes us special, makes perception
valuable—but it can also make us lonely. This loneliness
is different from being "alone." You can be lonely even
surrounded by people. The feeling I'm talking about stems
from the sense that we can never fully share the truth of
who we are. I experienced this acutely at an early age.

—AMY TAN

Father, we thank you for this day. Help us with
depression, loneliness, insecurity, low self-esteem, and
broken hearts. Grant us your healing power. Amen.

APRIL 25

Strength

He gives strength to the weary and
increases the power of the weak.
—ISAIAH 40:29 (NIV)

Every great dream begins with a dreamer. Always remember,
you have within you the strength, the patience, and the
passion to reach for the stars to change the world.
—HARRIET TUBMAN

Father, we are always grateful for each new day.
We are praying for a closer walk with you. For we
can do all things with your strength. Amen.

APRIL 26

Abundance

May God give you heaven's dew and earth's richness—
an abundance of grain and new wine.
—GENESIS 27:28 (NIV)

Whatever we are waiting for—peace of mind, contentment,
grace, the inner awareness of simple abundance—
it will surely come to us, but only when we are ready
to receive it with an open and grateful heart.
—SARAH BAN BREATHNACH

Father, we thank you for a life of abundance. We pray
never to take your gift for granted. Protect us from the
thief who comes to kill steal and destroy. Amen.

Love

If I speak in the tongues of men or of angels, but do not have love, I am only a resounding gong or a clanging cymbal. If I have the gift of prophecy and can fathom all mysteries and all knowledge, and if I have a faith that can move mountains, but do not have love, I am nothing. If I give all I possess to the poor and give over my body to hardship that I may boast, but do not have love, I gain nothing.

—1 CORINTHIANS 13:1–3 (NIV)

There is only one happiness in this life, to love and be loved.

—GEORGE SAND

Dear Father, we thank you for your love. We pray to love ourselves and others the way you love us. Love is patient, is kind, does not envy, is not self-seeking, and forgives. Amen.

APRIL 28

Healing

The men designated by name took the prisoners, and
from the plunder they clothed all who were naked. They
provided them with clothes and sandals, food and drink,
and healing balm. All those who were weak they put on
donkeys. So they took them back to their fellow Israelites
at Jericho, the City of Palms, and returned to Samaria.

—2 CHRONICLES 28:15 (NIV)

Did I offer peace today? Did I bring a smile to someone's
face? Did I say words of healing? Did I let go of my anger
and resentment? Did I forgive? Did I love? These are the real
questions. I must trust that the little bit of love that I sow now
will bear many fruits, here in this world and the life to come.

—HENRI NOUWEN

Dear Father, we thank you for your healing power.
We pray against all spirits causing diabetes, high blood
pressure, and heart, lung, and kidney diseases. Amen.

APRIL 29

Grace

For it is by grace you have been saved, through
faith—and this is not from yourselves, it is the gift of
God—not by works, so that no one can boast.

—EPHESIANS 2:8–9 (NIV)

Happiness cannot be traveled to, owned, earned, worn,
or consumed. Happiness is the spiritual experience of
living every minute with love, grace, and gratitude.

—DENIS WAITLEY

Father, we ask on this day for your mercy and grace. Help
us be more like you. Bless our families, friends, and loved
ones. Keep us safe on this day as we pray. Amen.

APRIL 30

Protection

Look, I have two daughters who have never slept with a
man. Let me bring them out to you, and you can do what
you like with them. But don't do anything to these men,
for they have come under the protection of my roof.

—GENESIS 19:8 (NIV)

I cannot think of any need in childhood as strong
as the need for a father's protection.

—SIGMUND FREUD

Dear Father, thank you for watching over us as we slept
last night. We pray for your guidance and protection.
Teach us patience and tolerance. Amen.

MAY 1

Grateful

But I, with shouts of grateful praise, will sacrifice
to you. What I have vowed, I will make good. I
will say, "Salvation comes from the Lord."
—JONAH 2:9 (NIV)

A grateful heart is a beginning of greatness. It is
an expression of humility. It is a foundation for the
development of such virtues as prayer, faith, courage,
contentment, happiness, love, and well-being.
— JAMES E. FAUST

Dear Father, we pray to be present in the moments of
this day, to be grateful for all your many blessings. Thank
you for sharing your precious love with us. Amen.

MAY 2

Daily Bread

Keep falsehood and lies far from me; give me neither
poverty nor riches, but give me only my daily bread.

—PROVERBS 30:8 (NIV)

Grace is available for each of us every day—our
spiritual daily bread—but we've got to remember to
ask for it with a grateful heart and not worry about
whether there will be enough for tomorrow.

—SARAH BAN BREATHNACH

Dear Father, thank you for the wake-up call. Give us this day our
daily bread. Forgive us our debts as we forgive our debtors. Amen.

MAY 3

Direct Our Footsteps

Direct my footsteps according to your word; let no sin rule over me. Redeem me from human oppression, that I may obey your precepts. Make your face shine on your servant and teach me your decrees.

—PSALM 119:133–135 (NIV)

So what do you desire to do? What do you really want to do as a person? You need to stop and document that; write it down; make a plan; and then God says, "I'll direct your steps."

—MYLES MUNROE

Father, thank you for this Friday. We are praying for your peace and understanding. We will walk in faith and let go of all fear. Direct our footsteps. Amen.

MAY 4

Grow Older

The Lord said to her, "Two nations are in your womb, and two peoples from within you will be separated; one people will be stronger than the other, and the older will serve the younger."

—GENESIS 25:23 (NIV)

You don't stop laughing because you grow older.
You grow older because you stop laughing.

—MAURICE CHEVALIER

Father, we thank you for our spiritual growth. As
we get older, we grow closer to you. As we work
out spiritually, you work with us. Amen.

MAY 5

Promises

For no matter how many promises God has made,
they are "Yes" in Christ. And so through him the
"Amen" is spoken by us to the glory of God.
—2 CORINTHIANS 1:20 (NIV)

Life is too short to worry about anything. You had better
enjoy it because the next day promises nothing.
—ERIC DAVIS

Almighty Father who has all power in heaven and
earth, thank you for your precious love and promises of
abundance. We stand on your Word today. Amen.

MAY 6

Renewing of Our Minds

Do not conform to the pattern of this world, but be transformed
by the renewing of your mind. Then you will be able to test and
approve what God's will is—his good, pleasing, and perfect will.

—ROMANS 12:2 (NIV)

We need to reject any politics that targets people because of
race or religion. This isn't a matter of political correctness.
It's a matter of understanding what makes us strong. The
world respects us not just for our arsenal; it respects us for our
diversity and our openness and the way we respect every faith.

—BARACK OBAMA

Almighty Father, we thank you for your creation. We
are praying for a renewing of our minds so that we can
understand your primary purpose for us. Amen.

MAY 7

Power

For I am not ashamed of the gospel, because it is the
power of God that brings salvation to everyone who
believes: first to the Jew, then to the Gentile.

—ROMANS 1:16 (NIV)

Every day we have plenty of opportunities to get angry, stressed or
offended. But what you're doing when you indulge these negative
emotions is giving something outside yourself power over your
happiness. You can choose to not let little things upset you.

—JOEL OSTEEN

Almighty Father, we glorify you on this day. Give us the desire
to obey you and the power to do what pleases you. Amen.

MAY 8

Abundance

But seven years of famine will follow them. Then
all the abundance in Egypt will be forgotten,
and the famine will ravage the land.
—GENESIS 41:30 (NIV)

Whatever we are waiting for—peace of mind, contentment,
grace, the inner awareness of simple abundance—
it will surely come to us, but only when we are ready
to receive it with an open and grateful heart.
—SARAH BAN BREATHNACH

Father, we thank you for this great connection with you.
Thank you for a life of abundance. We walk in faith love
and security because of your love for us. Amen.

MAY 9

Renewal of Our Minds

Do not conform to the pattern of this world, but be transformed by the renewing of your mind. Then you will be able to test and approve what God's will is—his good, pleasing, and perfect will.
—ROMANS 12:2 (NIV)

I've discovered that when we take time to renew our minds with God's Word, we learn how to think like God thinks, say what God says, and act like He wants us to act.
—JOYCE MEYER

Almighty Father, thank you for this day. We are praying for the renewal of our minds. Teach us things that will help us grow spiritually. Increase our faith in you. Amen.

MAY 10

Power of the Tongue

The tongue has the power of life and death,
and those who love it will eat its fruit.

—PROVERBS 18:21 (NIV)

You can change your world by changing your words ...
Remember, death and life are in the power of the tongue.

—JOEL OSTEEN

Father, we are grateful for this day. Thank you for the
power of the tongue. We speak positivity into our lives for
healing financial, family, and relationship issues. Amen.

MAY 11

Forgiveness

This is my blood of the covenant, which is poured
out for many for the forgiveness of sins.

—MATTHEW 26:28 (NIV)

Many times, the decisions we make affect and hurt your closest
friends and family the most. I have a lot of regrets in that regard.
But God has forgiven me, which I am very thankful for. It has
enabled me to forgive myself and move forward one day at a time.

—LEX LUGER

Father, thank you for this day. Please help us with patience
and humility. Show us how to forgive as we ask for
forgiveness. We let go and let you have your way. Amen.

MAY 12

Good Stewards

Therefore, since Christ suffered in his body, arm yourselves also
with the same attitude, because whoever suffers in the body is
done with sin. As a result, they do not live the rest of their earthly
lives for evil human desires, but rather for the will of God.

—1 PETER 4:1–2 (NIV)

If we're not a good steward of what God gives us, he takes it away.
I think that's what happened. I wasn't a good steward of the gift
that he gave me in this line of work. I abused it, so he took it away.

—SHAWN MICHAELS

Father, thank you for this day. We are grateful for all of
your many blessings down through the years. We are
praying to be good stewards of your many gifts. Amen.

MAY 13

Self-Discipline

For the Spirit God gave us does not make us timid,
but gives us power, love, and self-discipline.
—2 TIMOTHY 1:7 (NIV)

Work hard. Through determination and self-focus
and discipline, you can accomplish anything.
—KIMBERLY GUILFOYLE

Thank you, Father, for your grace. We are praying for
self-discipline and the power to rise above any situations
that are keeping us from moving forward. Amen.

Gentle Voice

After the earthquake came a fire, but the Lord was not
in the fire. And after the fire came a gentle whisper.
—1 KINGS 19:12 (NIV)

I think the first time I was ever really conscious of the difference
between people's voices was that my mother's voice was so
soft and gentle and her pronunciation was so perfect.
—MARIAN SELDES

Father God, we thank you for this day. We pray to stay
centered with you, allowing you to direct us. We want to
hear your gentle voice over the noise of this world. Amen.

MAY 15

Brokenness

My servants will sing out of the joy of their hearts, but you will
cry out from anguish of heart and wail in brokenness of spirit.
—ISAIAH 65:14 (NIV)

Brokenness is the operative issue of our time—
broken souls, broken hearts, broken places.
—SAMANTHA POWER

Father, thank you for this day. We pray for wholeness.
We pray for protection from broken marriages,
relationships, hearts, minds, and spirits. Amen.

New Mercies

Because of the Lord's great love we are not consumed,
for his compassions never fail. They are new
every morning; great is your faithfulness.
—LAMENTATIONS 3:22–23 (NIV)

God's mercy is fresh and new every morning.
—JOYCE MEYER

Father, we thank you for this day. We are grateful for
another week. We pray to stay focused, productive, and
progressive. Thank you for new mercies. Amen.

MAY 17

Traps

Then you may be sure that the Lord your God will no longer drive out these nations before you. Instead, they will become snares and traps for you, whips on your backs and thorns in your eyes, until you perish from this good land, which the Lord your God has given you.

—JOSHUA 23:13 (NIV)

Families rely on financial services more than ever, but those who need them most—who struggle to make ends meet—too often must contend with sky-high interest rates and tricks and traps buried in the fine print of their loan products.

—ELIZABETH WARREN

Father, we thank you for this day. Help us stay focused and consult you before making any major decisions. We pray not to fall into traps set to hinder us. Amen.

MAY 18

Fear

There is no fear in love. But perfect love drives out
fear, because fear has to do with punishment. The
one who fears is not made perfect in love.

—1 JOHN 4:18 (NIV)

Don't let fear or insecurity stop you from trying new
things. Believe in yourself. Do what you love. And most
importantly, be kind to others, even if you don't like them.

—STACY LONDON

Father, we are praying for our children on this day. Please
allow them to have full healthy lives without abuse,
fear, or lack. Shelter them from all danger. Amen.

MAY 19

Anxious

Do not be anxious about anything, but in
every situation, by prayer and petition, with
thanksgiving, present your requests to God.
—PHILIPPIANS 4:6 (NIV)

We should not fret for what is past, nor should we
be anxious about the future; men of discernment
deal only with the present moment.
—CHANAKYA

Thank you, Father, for another wake-up call. We are praying
not to be anxious or get ahead of you. Order our footsteps
in the directions you desire. We have faith in you. Amen.

MAY 20

Protection

But let all who take refuge in you be glad; let them ever sing for joy. Spread your protection over them, that those who love your name may rejoice in you.

—PSALM 5:11 (NIV)

Confidence ... thrives on honesty, on honor, on the sacredness of obligations, on faithful protection and on unselfish performance. Without them it cannot live.

—FRANKLIN D. ROOSEVELT

Dear Father, thank you for watching over us as we slept last night. We pray for your guidance and protection. Teach us patience and tolerance. Amen.

MAY 21

Confidence

So do not throw away your confidence; it will be richly rewarded.
—HEBREWS 10:35 (NIV)

Love is friendship that has caught fire. It is quiet
understanding, mutual confidence, sharing and forgiving. It
is loyalty through good and bad times. It settles for less than
perfection and makes allowances for human weaknesses.
—ANN LANDERS

Dear gracious Father, we thank you for this day. Please
prepare us face this day with confidence and assurance
that we can master this day with your help. Amen.

MAY 22

Focus

Fixing our eyes on Jesus, the pioneer and perfecter of faith.
For the joy set before him he endured the cross, scorning its
shame, and sat down at the right hand of the throne of God.

—HEBREWS 12:2 (NIV)

When you focus on being a blessing, God makes
sure that you are always blessed in abundance.

—JOEL OSTEEN

Dear Father, thank you for this day. We pray to live this
day to its fullest, not wasting time on things that don't
matter and focusing on the things that do. Amen.

MAY 23

Mistakes

We all stumble in many ways. Anyone who is never at fault in what they say is perfect, able to keep their whole body in check. When we put bits into the mouths of horses to make them obey us, we can turn the whole animal. Or take ships as an example. Although they are so large and are driven by strong winds, they are steered by a very small rudder wherever the pilot wants to go.

—JAMES 3:2–10 (NIV)

Take chances, make mistakes. That's how you grow. Pain nourishes your courage. You have to fail in order to practice being brave.

—MARY TYLER MOORE

Gracious Father, thank you for another day. We all fall short and make mistakes in life from time to time, but we thank you for giving us new mercies each day. Amen.

MAY 24

Healthy

No good tree bears bad fruit, nor does a bad tree bear good
fruit. Each tree is recognized by its own fruit. People do not
pick figs from thornbushes, or grapes from briers. A good man
brings good things out of the good stored up in his heart,
and an evil man brings evil things out of the evil stored up in
his heart. For the mouth speaks what the heart is full of.

—LUKE 6:43–45 (NIV)

Keep looking up! I learn from the past, dream
about the future, and look up. There's nothing
like a beautiful sunset to end a healthy day.

—RACHEL BOSTON

Father, we thank you for this day. We pray for
discipline to make healthy choices today and properly
nourish our bodies, minds, and spirits. Amen.

MAY 25

Courageous

Have I not commanded you? Be strong and courageous.
Do not be afraid; do not be discouraged, for the Lord
your God will be with you wherever you go.

—JOSHUA 1:9 (NIV)

He who is not courageous enough to take
risks will accomplish nothing in life.

—MUHAMMAD ALI

Dear Father, we thank you for this day. We pray to be courageous,
disciplined, productive, compassionate, and positive. Amen.

MAY 26

Blessings

The name of the righteous is used in blessings,
but the name of the wicked will rot.

—PROVERBS 10:7 (NIV)

Gratitude can transform common days into
thanksgivings, turn routine jobs into joy, and
change ordinary opportunities into blessings.

—WILLIAM ARTHUR WARD

Father, thank you for this day. We pray to never take your
many blessings for granted. Thank you for all things. Amen.

MAY 27

Increase

God blessed them and said, "Be fruitful and
increase in number and fill the water in the seas,
and let the birds increase on the earth."
—GENESIS 1:22 (NIV)

It turns out that advancing equal opportunity and economic
empowerment is both morally right and good economics,
because discrimination, poverty and ignorance restrict
growth, while investments in education, infrastructure
and scientific and technological research increase it,
creating more good jobs and new wealth for all of us.
—WILLIAM J. CLINTON

Thank you, Father, for this day. We pray for increases and
breakthroughs: financial, business, promotions. Amen.

Deliverance

But God sent me ahead of you to preserve for you a remnant
on earth and to save your lives by a great deliverance.

—GENESIS 45:7

The work of healing is not my work, but by faith, healing
is done. The work of deliverance, great and mighty
deliverance, is not my work but is my faith in Him. It is
not the works of righteousness which I have done, but
according to His grace. I am a product of His grace.

—T. B. JOSHUA

Dear Father, Creator of the heavens and earth, we are
praying for deliverance from the bondage of our past.
Help us move forward and not look backward. Amen.

MAY 29

Listen

Let the wise listen and add to their learning,
and let the discerning get guidance.
—PROVERBS 1:5 (NIV)

If people like you, they'll listen to you, but if they
trust you, they'll do business with you.
—ZIG ZIGLAR

Dear gracious Father, we thank you for giving us this day.
We are praying to listen to you more carefully and surrender
our will to you on this day. Keep us and guide us. Amen.

MAY 30

Strong

But God chose the foolish things of the world to shame the wise;
God chose the weak things of the world to shame the strong.
—1 CORINTHIANS 1:27 (NIV)

Work hard for what you want because it won't come to you
without a fight. You have to be strong and courageous and
know that you can do anything you put your mind to. If
somebody puts you down or criticizes you, just keep on
believing in yourself and turn it into something positive.
—LEAH LABELLE

Dear Father God, we are so grateful for this day. Please
hear our prayer. We are asking for your help to be stronger
and wiser. Help us make wise decisions. Amen.

Honor

"Honor your father and mother," which is the
first commandment with a promise.
—EPHESIANS 6:2 (NIV)

Our parents deserve our honor and respect for giving us life itself.
Beyond this they almost always made countless sacrifices as they
cared for and nurtured us through our infancy and childhood,
provided us with the necessities of life, and nursed us through
physical illnesses and the emotional stresses of growing up.

—EZRA TAFT BENSON

Dear Father God, we come to you as humble as we know how
to be, thanking you for this day. We pray to be the very best we
can be on this day and honor you in every possible way. Amen.

JUNE 1

Promise

The Lord is not slow in keeping his promise, as some understand
slowness. Instead he is patient with you, not wanting
anyone to perish, but everyone to come to repentance.

—2 PETER 3:9 (NIV)

It was that which gave promise that in due time the weights
should be lifted from the shoulders of all men, and that
all should have an equal chance. This is the sentiment
embodied in that Declaration of Independence.

—ABRAHAM LINCOLN

Father, we are grateful for this day and all that you have
done for us. We pray not to accept mediocrity, but to
live the life of abundance you promised us. Amen.

JUNE 2

Forgive

But if you do not forgive others their sins,
your Father will not forgive your sins.
—MATTHEW 6:15 (NIV)

I believe forgiveness is the best form of love in any
relationship. It takes a strong person to say they're
sorry and an even stronger person to forgive.
—YOLANDA HADID

Dear Father, thank you for one more day. We are
praying to do better than yesterday—more loving,
caring, forgiving, patient, and tolerant. Amen.

JUNE 3

Understanding

And the peace of God, which transcends all understanding, will guard your hearts and your minds in Christ Jesus.
—PHILIPPIANS 4:7 (NIV)

Love is friendship that has caught fire. It is quiet understanding, mutual confidence, sharing and forgiving. It is loyalty through good and bad times. It settles for less than perfection and makes allowances for human weaknesses.
—ANN LANDERS

Thank you, Father, for giving us a purpose-driven life. We pray for the understanding of that purpose and the power to carry it out. Amen.

JUNE 4

Relationship

No one has ever seen God, but the one and only Son,
who is himself God and is in closest relationship
with the Father, has made him known.

—JOHN 1:18 (NIV)

Nobody can predict the future. You just have to give your all to
the relationship you're in and do your best to take care of your
partner, communicate and give them every last drop of love you
have. I think one of the most important things in a relationship
is caring for your significant other through good times and bad.

—NICK CANNON

Dear Father, thank you for this day. We want to
improve our relationship with you. Show us your ways
and help us do the things that please you. Amen.

JUNE 5

Grateful

Sing to the Lord with grateful praise; make
music to our God on the harp.

—PSALM 147:7

A grateful heart is a beginning of greatness. It is
an expression of humility. It is a foundation for the
development of such virtues as prayer, faith, courage,
contentment, happiness, love, and well-being.

—JAMES E. FAUST

Dear Father, we thank you for this Monday the day
that you have prepared for us. We pray to do your
will and be grateful for all things. Amen.

JUNE 6

Unity

I in them and you in me—so that they may be brought to
complete unity. Then the world will know that you sent
me and have loved them even as you have loved me.

—JOHN 17:23 (NIV)

Neither man nor woman is perfect or complete without the
other. Thus, no marriage or family, no ward or stake is likely
to reach its full potential until husbands and wives, mothers
and fathers, men and women work together in unity of
purpose, respecting and relying upon each other's strengths.

—SHERI L. DEW

Dear Father, thank you for this Friday. We are
praying for peace, love, unity, forgiveness, patience,
joy, and happiness. We love you. Amen.

JUNE 7

Thoughtful

Fools find no pleasure in understanding but
delight in airing their own opinions.
—PROVERBS 18:2 (NIV)

This is the power of gathering: it inspires us, delightfully, to be
more hopeful, more joyful, more thoughtful: in a word, more alive.
—ALICE WATERS

Dear heavenly Father, we are grateful for this day. Help us
be thoughtful and a blessing to someone today. Amen.

JUNE 8

Illuminating

After this I saw another angel coming down from heaven. He had
great authority, and the earth was illuminated by his splendor.
—REVELATION 18:1 (NIV)

The lightbulb, the most humble and illuminating of all
technologies, when combined with a network connection,
transforms itself from being a bulb into a wake-up alarm, a mood
alteration mechanism, and in some cases, a cupid's assistant.
—OM MALIK

Dear Father, we are grateful for this day. We pray
to be the very best we can. Allow your spirit in
us to illuminate and attract others. Amen.

JUNE 9

Mercy

And may God Almighty grant you mercy before the man so that he will let your other brother and Benjamin come back with you. As for me, if I am bereaved, I am bereaved.

—GENESIS 43:14 (NIV)

It's easy to look at the things of this world to solve our challenges and obstacles in life, but when we submit our lives to Christ, His grace, mercy, peace, and love will bring true fulfillment to our lives.

—BETHANY HAMILTON

Merciful Father, we come to you on this day as humble as we know how to be. Hear our prayer for mercy for the immigrant children being separated from their parents. Amen.

JUNE 10

Family

This is the account of Noah and his family. Noah
was a righteous man, blameless among the people of
his time, and he walked faithfully with God.

—GENESIS 6:9 (NIV)

Learn to enjoy every minute of your life. Be happy now.
Don't wait for something outside of yourself to make
you happy in the future. Think how really precious is the
time you have to spend, whether it's at work or with your
family. Every minute should be enjoyed and savored.

—EARL NIGHTINGALE

Dear Father, we are grateful for this day. We pray
to stay focused and productive. Guide us through
this day. Bless our families and friends. Amen.

JUNE 11

Purpose

And we know that in all things God works for the good of those
who love him, who have been called according to his purpose.
—ROMANS 8:28 (NIV)

I truly believe that everything that we do and everyone that we
meet is put in our path for a purpose. There are no accidents;
we're all teachers—if we're willing to pay attention to the lessons
we learn, trust our positive instincts and not be afraid to take
risks or wait for some miracle to come knocking at our door.
—MARLA GIBBS

Father, thank you for this Friday. Thank you for
purpose in life. We are praying for self-respect and
honor. Create clean hearts in us. Amen.

JUNE 12

Fear

There is no fear in love. But perfect love drives out
fear, because fear has to do with punishment. The
one who fears is not made perfect in love.
—1 JOHN 4:18 (NIV)

You gain strength, courage, and confidence by every
experience in which you really stop to look fear in the
face. You are able to say to yourself, "I lived through this
horror. I can take the next thing that comes along."
—ELEANOR ROOSEVELT

Dear Father Almighty, we thank you for this
day. We are praying to live this day to its fullest,
letting go of all worries and fears. Amen.

JUNE 13

Unity

I in them and you in me—so that they may be brought to
complete unity. Then the world will know that you sent
me and have loved them even as you have loved me.

—JOHN 17:23 (NIV)

Neither man nor woman is perfect or complete without the
other. Thus, no marriage or family, no ward or stake is likely
to reach its full potential until husbands and wives, mothers
and fathers, men and women work together in unity of
purpose, respecting and relying upon each other's strengths.

—SHERI L. DEW

Good morning, Father. Thank you for this day. We
are praying for our families for peace, love, unity, and
forgiveness. Protect our children from harm. Amen.

JUNE 14

Expectation

For the creation waits in eager expectation for the children of God
to be revealed. For the creation was subjected to frustration, not by
its own choice, but by the will of the one who subjected it, in hope
that the creation itself will be liberated from its bondage to decay
and brought into the freedom and glory of the children of God.

—ROMANS 8:19–21 (NIV)

Make it a habit to tell people thank you. To express your
appreciation, sincerely and without the expectation of
anything in return. Truly appreciate those around you,
and you'll soon find many others around you. Truly
appreciate life, and you'll find that you have more of it.

—RALPH MARSTON

Dear Father, we come to you this day with great expectations.
Bless us financially with promotions, jobs, and businesses. Amen.

Temple

Do you not know that your bodies are temples of the
Holy Spirit, who is in you, whom you have received
from God? You are not your own; you were bought at
a price. Therefore honor God with your bodies.

—1 CORINTHIANS 6:19–20 (NIV)

The moment I have realized God sitting in the temple of every
human body, the moment I stand in reverence before every
human being and see God in him—that moment I am free
from bondage, everything that binds vanishes, and I am free.

—SWAMI VIVEKANANDA

Dear Father God, thank you for this day. We are praying for your
help to better take care of our bodies, minds, and spirits. Amen.

JUNE 16

Living Life

Since, then, you have been raised with Christ, set your
hearts on things above, where Christ is, seated at the right
hand of God. Set your minds on things above, not on
earthly things. For you died, and your life is now hidden
with Christ in God. When Christ, who is your life,
appears, then you also will appear with him in glory.

—COLOSSIANS 3:1–4

Cancer taught me to stop saving things for a special occasion.
Every day is special. You don't have to get cancer to start
living life to the fullest. My post-cancer philosophy? No
wasted time. No ugly clothes. No boring movies.

—REGINA BRETT

Almighty Father, thank you for this day. We are praying for
a God-centered day. Help us live life to its fullest and enjoy
this precious gift you have given us. We love you. Amen.

JUNE 17

Believe

Abram believed the Lord, and he credited
it to him as righteousness.
—GENESIS 15:6 (NIV)

Keep your dreams alive. Understand to achieve anything requires
faith and belief in yourself, vision, hard work, determination, and
dedication. Remember all things are possible for those who believe.
—GAIL DEVERS

Father, we sincerely thank you for all things. We pray
to feel your presence throughout this day. We believe
you will provide for our every need. Amen.

JUNE 18

Knowledge

The heart of the discerning acquires knowledge,
for the ears of the wise seek it out.
—PROVERBS 18:15 (NIV)

I would designate as science fiction in the best sense: they
are visions and anticipations by which we seek to attain a
true knowledge, but, in fact, they are only imaginations
whereby we seek to draw near to the reality.
—POPE BENEDICT XVI

Father, thank you for your creation, knowledge, and
wisdom. Help us with our unbelief. We know belief
and faith unlock the doors of knowledge. Amen.

JUNE 19

Character Defects

And you must not accept such animals from the
hand of a foreigner and offer them as the food of
your God. They will not be accepted on your behalf,
because they are deformed and have defects.

—LEVITICUS 22:25 (NIV)

My journey through life has led me through both light
and dark places, and it's because of those experiences
that I have learned how to work through my character
defects and to help others do the same.

—JESSIE PAVELKA

Father, thank you for the people in our lives who accept
us exactly where we are without judging us. We pray
to get better with our character defects. Amen.

JUNE 20

Needs

And my God will meet all your needs according
to the riches of his glory in Christ Jesus.
—PHILIPPIANS 4:19 (NIV)

We cannot seek achievement for ourselves and forget
about progress and prosperity for our community ... Our
ambitions must be broad enough to include the aspirations
and needs of others, for their sakes and for our own.
—CESAR CHAVEZ

Good morning, almighty Father God. We thank you
for this day. We are praying for all people. You know
all our needs—bless us on this day. Amen.

JUNE 21

Enemies

And praise be to God Most High, who delivered your enemies into your hand. Then Abram gave him a tenth of everything.

—GENESIS 14:20 (NIV)

It takes a great deal of bravery to stand up to our enemies, but just as much to stand up to our friends.

—J. K. ROWLING

Father, with your help, we come against the enemies within us: insecurity, self-centeredness, pride, jealousy, fear, anger, and envy. Amen.

JUNE 22

Positive Outcomes

Finally, brothers and sisters, whatever is true, whatever
is noble, whatever is right, whatever is pure, whatever is
lovely, whatever is admirable—if anything is excellent
or praiseworthy—think about such things.

—PHILIPPIANS 4:8 (NIV)

A positive attitude causes a chain reaction of
positive thoughts, events, and outcomes. It is a
catalyst and it sparks extraordinary results.

—WADE BOGGS

Dear heavenly Father, we thank you for another day. Please
show us how to be more productive and not waste time on
things that will not produce positive outcomes. Amen.

JUNE 23

Suffering

Not only so, but we also glory in our sufferings, because
we know that suffering produces perseverance.

—ROMANS 5:3 (NIV)

To live is to suffer, to survive is to find
some meaning in the suffering.

—FRIEDRICH NIETZSCHE

Dear Father God, we are grateful for another day.
We are praying for all those who are less fortunate
than ourselves. Bless the homeless and all those who
are suffering from lack in their lives. Amen.

JUNE 24

Kindness

But the fruit of the Spirit is love, joy, peace,
forbearance, kindness, goodness, faithfulness,

—GALATIANS 5:22 (NIV)

For beautiful eyes, look for the good in others; for
beautiful lips, speak only words of kindness; and for poise,
walk with the knowledge that you are never alone.

—AUDREY HEPBURN

Dear almighty God, we praise you and give all thanks to you
for your kindness and mercy and tender loving care. Please bless
us on this day with your guidance and protection. Amen.

Glory

Moses and Aaron then went into the tent of meeting.
When they came out, they blessed the people; and
the glory of the Lord appeared to all the people.
—LEVITICUS 9:23 (NIV)

There's no glory in climbing a mountain if all you want to do is to
get to the top. It's experiencing the climb itself—in all its moments
of revelation, heartbreak, and fatigue—that has to be the goal.

— KARYN KUSAMA

Dear Father, we come to you on this day with humble
hearts of thanksgiving. We thank you for all things—big
or small. We give you all the praise and glory. Amen.

Footsteps

Direct my footsteps according to your
word; let no sin rule over me.
—PSALM 119:133 (NIV)

God moves in a mysterious way, His wonders to perform. He
plants his footsteps in the sea, and rides upon the storm.
—WILLIAM COWPER

Dear God, we are so happy that you have spared us
to see another day. Please order our footsteps in the
direction you would have us go on this day. Amen.

JUNE 27

Change

⧼⧽

He who is the Glory of Israel does not lie or change his mind;
for he is not a human being, that he should change his mind.

—1 SAMUEL 15:29

Change your life today. Don't gamble on
the future, act now, without delay.

—SIMONE DE BEAUVOIR

Dear God, we are so grateful for another day. Please grant us
the serenity to accept the things we cannot change. Amen.

JUNE 28

Sickness

Worship the Lord your God, and his blessing will be on your food and water. I will take away sickness from among you.

—EXODUS 23:25 (NIV)

Prayer is an act of love; words are not needed. Even if sickness distracts from thoughts, all that is needed is the will to love.

—SAINT TERESA OF AVILA

Dear Father, we thank you for another wake-up call. We are praying for all those who are sick, in hospitals, having surgery and in nursing homes, suffering with pain in their bodies, minds, and spirits. Amen.

JUNE 29

Peace

I will grant peace in the land, and you will lie down and no one will make you afraid. I will remove wild beasts from the land, and the sword will not pass through your country.

—LEVITICUS 26:6 (NIV)

Peace is the beauty of life. It is sunshine. It is the smile of a child, the love of a mother, the joy of a father, the togetherness of a family. It is the advancement of man, the victory of a just cause, the triumph of truth.

—MENACHEM BEGIN

Dear God, we thank you for another day. We are praying for peace and understanding. Please guide us throughout this day and keep us protected from all harm and danger. Amen.

JUNE 30

Major Decisions

Also put the Urim and the Thummim in the breastpiece, so
they may be over Aaron's heart whenever he enters the presence
of the Lord. Thus Aaron will always bear the means of making
decisions for the Israelites over his heart before the Lord.

—EXODUS 28:30 (NIV)

It's much easier for me to make major life,
multimillion-dollar decisions, than it is to decide on
a carpet for my front porch. That's the truth.

—OPRAH WINFREY

Dear Father God, we come to you on this day with
thanksgiving in our hearts. Thanking you for all things.
We are praying today for your help to be stronger today
than we were yesterday. Help us stay focused and come
to you before we make any major decisions. Amen.

JULY · 1

Negative Forces

You bring new witnesses against me and increase your anger
toward me; your forces come against me wave upon wave.

—JOB 10:17 (NIV)

The demons are innumerable, appear at the most inconvenient
times, and create panic and terror. But I have learnt that
if I can master the negative forces and harness them to
my chariot, then they can work to my advantage.

—INGMAR BERGMAN

Dear God, thank you for this day. We are praying to be
positive and productive. Keep us aware of those negative,
draining forces that deplete our energy. Amen.

JULY 2

Shield

In addition to all this, take up the shield of faith, with which
you can extinguish all the flaming arrows of the evil one.
—EPHESIANS 6:16 (NIV)

Israel was not created in order to disappear—Israel
will endure and flourish. It is the child of hope and the
home of the brave. It can neither be broken by adversity
nor demoralized by success. It carries the shield of
democracy and it honors the sword of freedom.
Once you encounter people who are really testing
the limits of kindness, that's when you start to
build up a shield and close yourself down.
—MESHELL NDEGEOCELLO

Almighty Father, we are grateful for this new day. We
are praying for your help. Strengthen our minds and
shield us from negativity and procrastination. Amen.

JULY 3

Positive Energy

Finally, brothers and sisters, whatever is true, whatever
is noble, whatever is right, whatever is pure, whatever is
lovely, whatever is admirable—if anything is excellent
or praiseworthy—think about such things.

—PHILIPPIANS 4:8 (NIV)

We can bring positive energy into our daily lives by smiling
more, talking to strangers in line, replacing handshakes with
hugs, and calling our friends just to tell them we love them.

—BRANDON JENNER

Almighty Father, we thank you for this day and the
gift of love. We pray to be a blessing to someone
today by sharing positive energy. Amen.

JULY 4

Prayer

This, then, is how you should pray: "Our Father in heaven, hallowed be your name, your kingdom come, your will be done, on earth as it is in heaven. Give us today our daily bread."
—MATTHEW 6:19–13 (NIV)

A grateful heart is a beginning of greatness. It is an expression of humility. It is a foundation for the development of such virtues as prayer, faith, courage, contentment, happiness, love, and well-being.
—JAMES E. FAUST

Father, we are grateful for this day. Thank you for your love. Please guide and protect us from all harm. Bless our families and loved ones. Hear our prayers. Amen.

Cornerstone

So this is what the Sovereign Lord says: "See, I lay a stone in
Zion, a tested stone, a precious cornerstone for a sure foundation;
the one who relies on it will never be stricken with panic."
—ISAIAH 28:16 (NIV)

Democracy, pure democracy, has at least its foundation in a
generous theory of human rights. It is founded on the natural
equality of mankind. It is the cornerstone of the Christian
religion. It is the first element of all lawful government upon earth.
—JOHN QUINCY ADAMS

Thank you, Father, for this day. We pray to never sell out
our beliefs and principles. We know that character and
integrity are the cornerstones of an honorable life. Amen.

JULY 6

Masks

Therefore, since through God's mercy we have this ministry, we do not lose heart. Rather, we have renounced secret and shameful ways; we do not use deception, nor do we distort the word of God. On the contrary, by setting forth the truth plainly we commend ourselves to everyone's conscience in the sight of God. And even if our gospel is veiled, it is veiled to those who are perishing.

—2 CORINTHIANS 4 (NIV)

Love takes off masks that we fear we cannot live without and know we cannot live within.

—JAMES A. BALDWIN

Almighty Father, we are grateful for all things. We are praying for self-esteem. We want to be ourselves without the masks, accepting our assets and liabilities. Amen.

JULY 7

Calmness

If a ruler's anger rises against you, do not leave your
post; calmness can lay great offenses to rest.
—ECCLESIASTES 10:4 (NIV)

The more tranquil a man becomes, the greater is his
success, his influence, his power for good. Calmness
of mind is one of the beautiful jewels of wisdom.
—JAMES ALLEN

Thank you, Father, for the dawning of a new day.
We are praying for the spirit of calmness. Help us
replace fear with courage and faith. Amen.

JULY 8

Compassion

And the Lord said, "I will cause all my goodness to pass in
front of you, and I will proclaim my name, the Lord, in your
presence. I will have mercy on whom I will have mercy, and
I will have compassion on whom I will have compassion."
—EXODUS 33:19 (NIV)

Mama was my greatest teacher, a teacher of compassion,
love, and fearlessness. If love is sweet as a flower,
then my mother is that sweet flower of love.
—STEVIE WONDER

Dear Father God of compassion and comfort, we thank
you for loving us the way you do. We are praying to be
the same way with others as you are with us. Amen.

Dreams

As when a hungry person dreams of eating, but awakens hungry still; as when a thirsty person dreams of drinking, but awakens faint and thirsty still. So will it be with the hordes of all the nations that fight against Mount Zion.

—ISAIAH 29:8 (NIV)

Every great dream begins with a dreamer. Always remember, you have within you the strength, the patience, and the passion to reach for the stars to change the world.

—HARRIET TUBMAN

Almighty Father, we are so grateful for this day. Our prayer is that we let go of all fear and anxiety and pursue the dreams we once had. Let us not be sleepwalkers of life. Amen.

Creator

So then, those who suffer according to God's will should commit themselves to their faithful Creator and continue to do good.
—1 PETER 4:19 (NIV)

When I admire the wonders of a sunset or the beauty of the moon, my soul expands in the worship of the creator.
—MAHATMA GANDHI

Almighty God, thank you for creating us. We all are in you—and you are all in us. We are praying for wisdom and understanding of your power within us. Amen.

JULY 11

Closer Walk

"Do not come any closer," God said. "Take off your sandals,
for the place where you are standing is holy ground."
—EXODUS 3:5 (NIV)

I realized that my grandfather walked with Martin Luther
King forty years ago. That was his dream. And in his little
way, he helped us get closer to where we are today.
—TIM DALY

Dear Father, thank you for this day. We are praying for
a closer walk and personal time with you, not letting the
busyness of this day take priority over you. Amen.

JULY 12

Orderly

But everything should be done in a fitting and orderly way.
—1 CORINTHIANS 14:40 (NIV)

To love rightly is to love what is orderly and
beautiful in an educated and disciplined way.
—PLATO

Almighty Father, Creator of the universe, we are grateful
for another week. We are praying for good orderly
direction (GOD). Order our steps today. Amen.

JULY 13

Guidance

For lack of guidance a nation falls, but victory
is won through many advisers.
—PROVERBS 11:14 (NIV)

Be true to yourself, help others, make each day your masterpiece,
make friendship a fine art, drink deeply from good books—
especially the Bible, build a shelter against a rainy day, give
thanks for your blessings, and pray for guidance every day.
—JOHN WOODEN

Almighty Creator, we are extremely grateful for
this day. Please continue to guide provide and
protect us. We give you all the praise. Amen.

JULY 14

Enemy Schemes

He catches the wise in their craftiness, and the
schemes of the wily are swept away.
—JOB 5:13 (NIV)

The mind is never satisfied with the objects immediately
before it, but is always breaking away from the present
moment, and losing itself in schemes of future felicity …
The natural flights of the human mind are not from
pleasure to pleasure, but from hope to hope.
—SAMUEL JOHNSON

Dear God, thank you for waking us up this morning. We
are praying for your help to have more faith than fear.
Protect our minds from the enemy's schemes. Amen.

JULY 15

Deliverance

You are my hiding place; you will protect me from
trouble and surround me with songs of deliverance.

—PSALM 32:7 (NIV)

The work of healing is not my work, but by faith, healing
is done. The work of deliverance, great and mighty
deliverance, is not my work but is my faith in Him. It is
not the works of righteousness which I have done, but
according to His grace. I am a product of His grace.

—T. B. JOSHUA

Thank you, Father, for this day. We are praying for
deliverance from the bondages of our past so that we
can fulfill our purposes in life to its fullest. Amen.

Healing

Jesus went through all the towns and villages, teaching
in their synagogues, proclaiming the good news of the
kingdom, and healing every disease and sickness.

—MATTHEW 9:35 (NIV)

Did I offer peace today? Did I bring a smile to someone's
face? Did I say words of healing? Did I let go of my anger
and resentment? Did I forgive? Did I love? These are the real
questions. I must trust that the little bit of love that I sow now
will bear many fruits, here in this world and the life to come.

—HENRI NOUWEN

Good morning, Father. We are blessed to see this day. We
are praying for healing. We rebuke and cast out any spirit
of cancer: skin, lung, liver, pancreas, or kidney. Amen.

JULY 17

Gifts and Talents

Again, it will be like a man going on a journey, who called his servants and entrusted his wealth to them. To one he gave five bags of gold, to another two bags, and to another one bag, each according to his ability. Then he went on his journey. The man who had received five bags of gold went at once and put his money to work and gained five bags more.

—MATTHEW 25:14–30 (NIV)

I was blessed with certain gifts and talents and God gave them to me to be the best person I can be and to have a positive impact on other people.

—BRYAN CLAY

Dear Father God, thank you for this new week. We are praying to be productive and creative. Help us use the gifts and talents you have given us wisely. Amen.

JULY 18

Self-Discipline

For the Spirit God gave us does not make us timid,
but gives us power, love, and self-discipline.
—2 TIMOTHY 1:7 (NIV)

Self-discipline is an act of cultivation. It requires you to connect
today's actions to tomorrow's results. There's a season for sowing a
season for reaping. Self-discipline helps you know which is which.
—GARY RYAN BLAIR

Dear Father God, we thank you for this Friday. We
are praying for self-discipline and the power to rise
above life situations that are hindering us. Amen.

Care

The warden paid no attention to anything under
Joseph's care, because the Lord was with Joseph
and gave him success in whatever he did.

—GENESIS 39:23 (NIV)

Nobody can predict the future. You just have to give your all to
the relationship you're in and do your best to take care of your
partner, communicate and give them every last drop of love you
have. I think one of the most important things in a relationship
is caring for your significant other through good times and bad.

—NICK CANNON

Dear Father, thank you for this day. We are so grateful
for all things big or small. We pray to show our gratitude
in the way we care and share with others. Amen.

JULY 20

Improvement

We who are strong ought to bear with the failings of the weak and not to please ourselves. Each of us should please our neighbors for their good, to build them up. For even Christ did not please himself but, as it is written: "The insults of those who insult you have fallen on me."
—ROMANS 15:1–3 (NIV)

Without continual growth and progress, such words as improvement, achievement, and success have no meaning.
—BENJAMIN FRANKLIN

Father God, we thank you for another day among the living. We pray to improve our eating and exercising habits. With your help, we can be healthier. Amen.

JULY 21

Procrastination

A sluggard's appetite is never filled, but the
desires of the diligent are fully satisfied.
—PROVERBS 13:4 (NIV)

Procrastination is one of the most common and deadliest of
diseases, and its toll on success and happiness is heavy.
—WAYNE GRETZKY

Dear heavenly Father, thank you for this day. We are
praying to you for guidance. Help us stay focused and
productive. We bind the spirit of procrastination. Amen.

JULY 22

Grace

For it is by grace you have been saved, through
faith—and this is not from yourselves, it is the gift of
God— not by works, so that no one can boast.

—EPHESIANS 2:8–9 (NIV)

Sometimes we may ask God for success, and He gives us physical
and mental stamina. We might plead for prosperity, and we receive
enlarged perspective and increased patience, or we petition for
growth and are blessed with the gift of grace. He may bestow upon
us conviction and confidence as we strive to achieve worthy goals.

—DAVID A. BEDNAR

Dear Father, we thank you for your grace. It's your grace
that has saved us. We thank you for your Son, Jesus Christ,
who died for our sins. We love and magnify you. Amen.

JULY 23

Salvation

The Lord is my strength and my defense; he has become my salvation. He is my God, and I will praise him, my father's God, and I will exalt him.

—EXODUS 15:2 (NIV)

When it comes to my salvation, all I need is Jesus; after my salvation, everything is Jesus plus the church … When people preach that all you need is Jesus, they cut you and I off from one of the greatest sources of healing, which is the body of Christ. Don't go it alone—you won't make it.

—JOSH MCDOWELL

Dear Father, who art in heaven, we thank you for being our strength and defense. You are our salvation, and we will continue to praise you and give you all the glory. Amen.

Mountaintop

Moses removed Aaron's garments and put them on his son
Eleazar. And Aaron died there on top of the mountain.
Then Moses and Eleazar came down from the mountain.

—NUMBERS 20:28 (NIV)

Only when you drink from the river of silence shall you
indeed sing. And when you have reached the mountain
top, then you shall begin to climb. And when the earth
shall claim your limbs, then shall you truly dance.

—KHALIL GIBRAN

Dear God, we thank you for our mountaintop experiences. We
are praying today to never get ahead of you, for you know what
is best for us and the time and place for everything. Amen.

Promise

The Lord is not slow in keeping his promise, as some understand
slowness. Instead he is patient with you, not wanting
anyone to perish, but everyone to come to repentance.

—2 PETER 3:9 (NIV)

Now, as a nation, we don't promise equal outcomes, but we were
founded on the idea everybody should have an equal opportunity
to succeed. No matter who you are, what you look like, where
you come from, you can make it. That's an essential promise of
America. Where you start should not determine where you end up.

—BARACK OBAMA

Dear Father, we thank you for this day. We pray to never
take you or your promises for granted. Please forgive
us for our many sins through the years. Amen.

JULY 26

Light

God called the light "day," and the darkness he called "night."
And there was evening, and there was morning—the first day.
—GENESIS 1:5 (NIV)

When you rise in the morning, give thanks for the light, for your
life, for your strength. Give thanks for your food and for the joy of
living. If you see no reason to give thanks, the fault lies in yourself.
—TECUMSEH

Dear Father, we thank you for your creation. We
thank you for the dawning of each and every new
morning. We love you and adore you. Amen.

Ambition

For where you have envy and selfish ambition, there
you find disorder and every evil practice.

—JAMES 3:16 (NIV)

Character cannot be developed in ease and quiet. Only
through experience of trial and suffering can the soul be
strengthened, ambition inspired, and success achieved.

—HELEN KELLER

Dear gracious Father, we come before you on this day with
thanksgiving in our hearts. We pray that our ambition is
not selfish. We try to be selfless. Please give us wisdom and
the knowledge to complete the tasks before us. Amen.

JULY 28

Justice

When justice is done, it brings joy to the
righteous but terror to evildoers.

—PROVERBS 21:15 (NIV)

In the real world, as lived and experienced by real people,
the demand for human rights and dignity, the longing
for liberty and justice and opportunity, the hatred of
oppression and corruption and cruelty is reality.

—JOHN MCCAIN

Dear Father God, we thank you for another day. We
are praying to be righteous on this day, not perfect
which is impossible for humans. We are praying for
justice for the evildoers of this world. Amen.

Peace

Do not suppose that I have come to bring peace to the earth.
I did not come to bring peace, but a sword. For I have come
to turn "a man against his father, a daughter against her
mother, a daughter-in-law against her mother-in-law— a
man's enemies will be the members of his own household."
—MATTHEW 10:34–36 (NIV)

Gratitude makes sense of our past, brings peace
for today, and creates a vision for tomorrow.
—MELODY BEATTIE

Dear Father, we are so grateful for another day. We
are praying to better than we were on yesterday.
Grant us your peace, mercy, and grace. Amen.

JULY 30

Joy

But the fruit of the Spirit is love, joy, peace,
forbearance, kindness, goodness, faithfulness.
—GALATIANS 5:22 (NIV)

Today I choose life. Every morning when I wake up I can choose
joy, happiness, negativity, pain … To feel the freedom that comes
from being able to continue to make mistakes and choices—today
I choose to feel life, not to deny my humanity but embrace it.
—KEVYN AUCOIN

Dear Father, we thank you for another day. We are
praying to be pleasing unto to on this day. Bless us with
your joy which is beyond understanding. Amen.

JULY 31

Help

Adam made love to his wife Eve, and she became
pregnant and gave birth to Cain. She said, "With the
help of the Lord, I have brought forth a man."
—GENESIS 4:1 (NIV)

Be true to yourself, help others, make each day your masterpiece,
make friendship a fine art, drink deeply from good books—
especially the Bible, build a shelter against a rainy day, give
thanks for your blessings and pray for guidance every day.
—JOHN WOODEN

Dear Father, we thank you for another day in your grace. We are
praying for help for all those who are really struggling with life
and its challenges. Grant them a peace of mind and hope. Amen.

AUGUST 1

Guidance

For lack of guidance a nation falls, but victory
is won through many advisers.
—PROVERBS 11:14 (NIV)

Spirituality can release blocks, lead you to ideas, and make your
life artful. Sometimes when we pray for guidance, we're guided
in unexpected directions. We may want a lofty answer and we get
the intuition to clean our bedroom. It can seem so humble and
picky and that you don't necessarily think of its spiritual guidance.
—JULIA CAMERON

Dear Father God, we are grateful for this day. Please be with and
guide our family, friends, and coworkers on this day. Amen.

Unconfessed Sins

He went into all the country around the Jordan, preaching
a baptism of repentance for the forgiveness of sins.

—LUKE 3:3 (NIV)

I often remembered also that I had been told, that we
shall have as many devils biting us, if we go to hell,
as we have unconfessed sins on our consciences.

—MARIA MONK

Dear Father God, we thank you for another day. We
pray to be better than yesterday. Please forgive us for
any unconfessed sins, for we have all fallen short of your
glory. Thank you for your grace and mercy. Amen.

AUGUST 3

Holy Spirit

But the Advocate, the Holy Spirit, whom the Father
will send in my name, will teach you all things and
will remind you of everything I have said to you.

—JOHN 14:26 (NIV)

Many people feel so pressured by the expectations of others
that it causes them to be frustrated, miserable and confused
about what they should do. But there is a way to live a simple,
joy-filled, peaceful life, and the key is learning how to be led
by the Holy Spirit, not the traditions or expectations of man.

—JOYCE MEYER

Good morning, Holy Spirit. Father, we thank you for your spirit
that lives within us. We are praying for a deeper understanding
of how to utilize the power you have given us. Amen.

AUGUST 4

Smile

The Lord bless you and keep you; the Lord make his
face shine on you and be gracious to you; the Lord
turn his face toward you and give you peace.

—NUMBERS 6:24–26 (NIV)

Peace is the beauty of life. It is sunshine. It is the smile
of a child, the love of a mother, the joy of a father, the
togetherness of a family. It is the advancement of man,
the victory of a just cause, the triumph of truth.

—MENACHEM BEGIN

Frown—and you frown alone. Smile—and the world
smiles with you. Dear Father, we thank you for this day.
We pray to smile and have more laughter in our lives.
Laughter can be healing and contagious. Amen.

AUGUST 5

Harm

You intended to harm me, but God intended it for good to
accomplish what is now being done, the saving of many lives.
—GENESIS 50:20 (NIV)

All mankind … being all equal and independent, no one ought
to harm another in his life, health, liberty, or possessions.
—JOHN LOCKE

Dear Father, we thank you for this day. We first give honor
to you for all things. We are praying to be our very best on
this day. Please guide us in the direction you desire. Let us be
careful not to harm anyone, especially ourselves. Amen.

AUGUST 6

Daily Bread

Keep falsehood and lies far from me; give me neither
poverty nor riches, but give me only my daily bread.
—PROVERBS 30:8 (NIV)

Grace is available for each of us every day—our
spiritual daily bread—but we've got to remember to
ask for it with a grateful heart and not worry about
whether there will be enough for tomorrow.
—SARAH BAN BREATHNACH

Thank you, Father, for this Friday. We honor and praise you.
Give us this day our daily bread. Draw us closer to you—and
teach us to be doers of your Word. We pray for our children.
Help us be positive influences in their lives by talking the
talk *and* walking the walk of righteousness. Amen.

AUGUST 7

Stewards

Each of you should use whatever gift you have received to serve others, as faithful stewards of God's grace in its various forms.
—1 PETER 4:10 (NIV)

Nature surrounds us, from parks and backyards to streets and alleyways. Next time you go out for a walk, tread gently and remember that we are both inhabitants and stewards of nature in our neighborhoods.
—DAVID SUZUK

Dear Father, we thank you for this day. We are praying for your help. Life is short even at its longest. Help us be all that you created us to be. Strengthen our minds so that we may stay focused and be progressive and good stewards with the many gifts you have given us. Amen.

AUGUST 8

Pride

Pride goes before destruction, a haughty spirit before a fall.
—PROVERBS 16:18 (NIV)

It was pride that changed angels into devils; it
is humility that makes men as angels.
—SAINT AUGUSTINE

Dear God—our Father, Creator of the universe—we come
before you on this day with thanksgiving in our hearts. We
desire to be more like you. Help us rid ourselves of fear, anger,
resentments, envy, jealousy, and pride. Help us replace them
with faith, forgiveness, compassion, patience, and love. Amen.

AUGUST 9

Weakness

But he said to me, "My grace is sufficient for you, for
my power is made perfect in weakness." Therefore I
will boast all the more gladly about my weaknesses,
so that Christ's power may rest on me.

—2 CORINTHIANS 12:9 (NIV)

Our greatest weakness lies in giving up. The most certain
way to succeed is always to try just one more time.

—THOMAS A. EDISON

Dear heavenly Father, we are so grateful for this day. We take this
time to get centered with you. Help us grow in the areas that need
growth. Strengthen us where we are weak. Use us as blessings for
others on this day. We give you all the praise and glory. Amen.

AUGUST 10

Productive

Again, it will be like a man going on a journey, who called
his servants and entrusted his wealth to them. To one he
gave five bags of gold, to another two bags, and to another
one bag, each according to his ability. Then he went on his
journey. The man who had received five bags of gold went at
once and put his money to work and gained five bags more.

MATTHEW 25:14–30 (NIV)

As long as your intentions are solid and about growth
and progression and being productive and not being
idle, then you're doing good in my book.

—FRANK OCEAN

Dear Father God, thank you for this new week. We are
praying for your guidance. Help us be productive and
creative. Show us how to let go of yesterday's failures and
focus on today's promises and opportunities. Amen.

AUGUST 11

Humble Spirit

Has not my hand made all these things, and so they came into being?" declares the Lord. "These are the ones I look on with favor: those who are humble and contrite in spirit, and who tremble at my word.
—ISAIAH 66:2 (NIV)

You often feel that your prayers scarcely reach the ceiling; but, oh, get into this humble spirit by considering how good the Lord is, and how evil you all are, and then prayer will mount on wings of faith to heaven.
—CHARLES SIMEON

Father, thank you for this day. You said in your Word: "When a believing person prays, great things happen" (James 5:16). We are praying today for good health, financial blessings, and a humble spirit. We pray this prayer with great expectations. Amen.

AUGUST 12

All in All

Then God said, "Let us make mankind in our image, in our likeness, so that they may rule over the fish in the sea and the birds in the sky, over the livestock and all the wild animals, and over all the creatures that move along the ground."
—GENESIS 1:26 (NIV)

Christ is in all, meaning that the divine spark is in all things.
—TOM SHADYAC

Dear heavenly Father, we are grateful for this day. We are praying to stay focused and productive. Help us see you in everything, for you are all, and all is in you. Amen.

AUGUST 13

Complaining

Do everything without grumbling or arguing.
—PHILIPPIANS 2:14 (NIV)

What we need to do is always lean into the future; when the world
changes around you and when it changes against you—what used
to be a tailwind is now a headwind—you have to lean into that
and figure out what to do because complaining isn't a strategy.
—JEFF BEZOS

Dear Father, thank you for this day. We are praying
to be more grateful for what we have and to stop
complaining about what we don't have. Amen.

AUGUST 14

Consideration

Regard them as holy, because they offer up the
food of your God. Consider them holy, because I
the Lord am holy—I who make you holy.
—LEVITICUS 21:8 (NIV)

Dreams are the guiding words of the soul. Why should
I henceforth not love my dreams and not make their
riddling images into objects of my daily consideration?
—CARL JUNG

Almighty Father, we thank you again for this day. We are
praying to be more like you: loving, kind, considerate,
forgiving, patient, peaceful, and compassionate. Amen.

AUGUST 15

Adore

Take me away with you—let us hurry! Let the king bring me into his chambers. We rejoice and delight in you; we will praise your love more than wine. How right they are to adore you!

—SONG OF SONGS 1:4 (NIV)

In prayer, we stand where angels bow with veiled faces. There, even there, the cherubim and seraphim adore before that selfsame throne to which our prayers ascend. And shall we come there with stunted requests and narrow, contracted faith?

—CHARLES SPURGEON

Dear Father, we are thankful for this Monday. We are praying to keep gratitude in our attitudes because you're so good to us. We love and adore you. Amen.

AUGUST 16

Learning Experiences

Instruct the wise and they will be wiser still; teach the
righteous and they will add to their learning.
—PROVERBS 9:9 (NIV)

There is only one thing more painful than learning from
experience and that is not learning from experience.
—ARCHIBALD MACLEISH

Thank you, Father, for this day. We understand that,
without adversity, we would never develop wisdom, and
without wisdom, success would be short-lived indeed.
Thank you for life-learning experiences. Amen.

AUGUST 17

Forgiveness

This is my blood of the covenant, which is poured
out for many for the forgiveness of sins.
—MATTHEW 26:28 (NIV)

There is no love without forgiveness, and
there is no forgiveness without love.
—BRYANT H. MCGILL

Father God, we are grateful for this day. Thank you for your
grace and mercy. We are praying to forgive others as you
have forgiven us. Help us move forward in life. Amen.

AUGUST 18

Gentleness

Let your gentleness be evident to all. The Lord is near.
—PHILIPPIANS 4:5 (NIV)

A Christian reveals true humility by showing the gentleness
of Christ, by being always ready to help others, by speaking
kind words and performing unselfish acts, which elevate and
ennoble the most sacred message that has come to our world.
—ELLEN G. WHITE

Thank you, Father, for this day. We are praying to be blessings
for someone else today, sharing a kind word, a gentle smile,
or encouragement—without any expectations. Amen.

AUGUST 19

God-Centered Living

Whenever the rainbow appears in the clouds, I will see
it and remember the everlasting covenant between God
and all living creatures of every kind on the earth.

—GENESIS 9:16 (NIV)

For the Puritans, the God-centered life meant making the quest
for spiritual and moral holiness the great business of life.

—LELAND RYKEN

Good morning, Father. Thank you for this day. We are
praying to get totally centered with you as we start this day.
Be our guide and keep us safe from all harm. Amen.

Improvements

We who are strong ought to bear with the failings of the weak and not to please ourselves. Each of us should please our neighbors for their good, to build them up. For even Christ did not please himself but, as it is written: "The insults of those who insult you have fallen on me."

—ROMANS 15:1–3 (NIV)

Never be afraid to fail. Failure is only a stepping stone to improvement. Never be overconfident because that will block your improvement.

—TONY JAA

Father, we are grateful for another week. Thank you for the lessons of last week. We pray for improvements in our lives and more conscious contact with you. Amen.

AUGUST 21

Direction

Trust in the Lord with all your heart and lean not
on your own understanding; in all your ways submit
to him, and he will make your paths straight.

—PROVERBS 3:5–6 (NIV)

As you keep your mind and heart focused in the right
direction, approaching each day with faith and gratitude,
I believe you will be empowered to live life to the fullest
and enjoy the abundant life He has promised you!

—VICTORIA OSTEEN

Dear Father, thank you for this day. We are praying for those
who suffer from depression, low self-esteem, loneliness, or
lack of direction in life. Fill the gap for them. Amen.

Increases

He gives strength to the weary and
increases the power of the weak.

—ISAIAH 40:29 (NIV)

On the relationship side, if you teach people to respond
actively and constructively when someone they care
about has a victory, it increases love and friendship
and decreases the probability of depression.

—MARTIN SELIGMAN

Father, we humble ourselves before you on this day. Thank
you for your grace, mercy, and favor. We are praying for
increases in our lives. Let your will be done. Amen.

AUGUST 23

Attitude

May the God who gives endurance and encouragement give you
the same attitude of mind toward each other that Christ Jesus had.

—ROMANS 15:5 (NIV)

I believe if you keep your faith, you keep your trust, you keep the
right attitude, if you're grateful, you'll see God open up new doors.

—JOEL OSTEEN

Dear Father, we are truly grateful for this day. We are
praying for an attitude of gratitude. Thank you for providing
for all of our needs and many of our wants. Amen.

AUGUST 24

Desire

Take delight in the Lord, and he will give
you the desires of your heart.

—PSALM 37:4 (NIV)

Desire is the key to motivation, but it's determination
and commitment to an unrelenting pursuit of your
goal—a commitment to excellence—that will
enable you to attain the success you seek.

—MARIO ANDRETTI

Dear Father God, we thank you for another day. We are
praying for your guidance. Order our footsteps in the
direction you desire for us—in the name of Jesus. Amen.

AUGUST 25

Peace

I will grant peace in the land, and you will lie down and no
one will make you afraid. I will remove wild beasts from the
land, and the sword will not pass through your country.

—LEVITICUS 26:6 (NIV)

Peace is the beauty of life. It is sunshine. It is the smile
of a child, the love of a mother, the joy of a father, the
togetherness of a family. It is the advancement of man,
the victory of a just cause, the triumph of truth.

—MENACHEM BEGIN

Dear God, we are so grateful for another day. We are praying for
world peace. Help us love one another instead of hating, envying,
and destroying each other. In the name of Jesus, we pray. Amen.

AUGUST 26

Praise

Give praise to the Lord, proclaim his name; make
known among the nations what he has done.

—1 CHRONICLES 16:8 (NIV)

Glory be and praise to God. I didn't do any of this. God
did. I don't have a recipe or a blueprint. I prayed for it,
and my prayers are continuing to be answered.

—KEVIN GATES

Dear God, we come to you this day with thanksgiving in
our hearts. We give you all the praise and honor. Thank
you for loving us the way you do. We love you. Amen.

AUGUST 27

Appreciation

rooted and built up in him, strengthened in the faith as
you were taught, and overflowing with thankfulness.

—COLOSSIANS 2:7 (NIV)

Make it a habit to tell people thank you. To express your
appreciation, sincerely and without the expectation of
anything in return. Truly appreciate those around you,
and you'll soon find many others around you. Truly
appreciate life, and you'll find that you have more of it.

—RALPH MARSTON

Dear God, we thank you for this day. We are praying today for
our family, friends, and loved ones. Help us be more appreciative
of each other and to not take this life for granted. Amen.

Mercy

And the Lord said, "I will cause all my goodness to pass in
front of you, and I will proclaim my name, the Lord, in your
presence. I will have mercy on whom I will have mercy, and
I will have compassion on whom I will have compassion."
—EXODUS 33:19 (NIV)

God's mercy is fresh and new every morning.
—JOYCE MEYER

Dear God, we come to you on this day with hearts of gratitude.
You have been so merciful. Thank you for forgiving us for our
many sins. We are praying to do better in our lives. Amen.

AUGUST 29

Temptation

Watch and pray so that you will not fall into temptation.
The spirit is willing, but the flesh is weak.

—MATTHEW 26:41 (NIV)

Darkness comes. In the middle of it, the future looks
blank. The temptation to quit is huge. Don't. You are in
good company ... You will argue with yourself that there
is no way forward. But with God, nothing is impossible.
He has more ropes and ladders and tunnels out of pits than
you can conceive. Wait. Pray without ceasing. Hope.

—JOHN PIPER

Dear Father, we thank you for this day. Please help
us with our temptation on this day. We surrender our
wills to you. Please give us peace of mind. We know
you will help us when we call on you. Amen.

AUGUST 30

Power

For I am not ashamed of the gospel, because it is the
power of God that brings salvation to everyone who
believes: first to the Jew, then to the Gentile.

—ROMANS 1:16 (NIV)

Human greatness does not lie in wealth or power, but in character
and goodness. People are just people, and all people have faults
and shortcomings, but all of us are born with a basic goodness.

—ANNE FRANK

Dear Father God, we are weak—but you are strong. We
are praying for the full understanding of the power you
have given us as your children. Open our minds to receive
the power of the truth so that we may take authority
over the things that are holding us down. Amen.

AUGUST 31

Grace

For it is by grace you have been saved, through
faith—and this is not from yourselves, it is the gift of
God— not by works, so that no one can boast.

—EPHESIANS 2:8–9 (NIV)

Sometimes we may ask God for success, and He gives us physical
and mental stamina. We might plead for prosperity, and we receive
enlarged perspective and increased patience, or we petition for
growth and are blessed with the gift of grace. He may bestow upon
us conviction and confidence as we strive to achieve worthy goals.

—DAVID A. BEDNAR

Dear gracious Father, we come to you this day thanking
you for all things, big and small. Please continue
to bless us with your mercy and grace. Help us stay
focused on this day and be productive. Amen.

SEPTEMBER 1

Protection

But let all who take refuge in you be glad; let them
ever sing for joy. Spread your protection over them that
those who love your name may rejoice in you.

—PSALM 5:11 (NIV)

Protection of religious freedom means considering
the faiths and beliefs of everyone involved.

—MIKE QUIGLEY

Dear Father, we thank you for this day. We are praying for
our children. Keep them safe from all harm and danger.
Put a hedge of protection around them. Amen.

SEPTEMBER 2

Achievements

Dear friends, do not believe every spirit, but test the
spirits to see whether they are from God, because many
false prophets have gone out into the world.

—1 JOHN 4:1 (NIV)

Achievements are precious and timeless, just like the
precious metal platinum. And what better way to celebrate
milestones in your life than with precious platinum.

—VIJENDER SINGH

Dear Father, help us understand that strife and
struggles can inspire us to overcome adversity and
propel us into real achievements. Amen.

Judgment

Therefore, say to the Israelites: "I am the Lord, and I will bring
you out from under the yoke of the Egyptians. I will free
you from being slaves to them, and I will redeem you with
an outstretched arm and with mighty acts of judgment."

—EXODUS 6:6 (NIV)

Depend upon yourself. Make your judgment trustworthy by
trusting it. You can develop good judgement as you do the
muscles of your body—by judicious, daily exercise. To be known
as a man of sound judgement will be much in your favor.

—GRANTLAND RICE

Dear God, help us keep the focus on ourselves and not
be judgmental of others. We all have character defects.
We are praying to get better with your help. Amen.

SEPTEMBER 4

Challenges

The Pharisees and some of the teachers of the law who had come from Jerusalem gathered around Jesus and saw some of his disciples eating food with hands that were defiled, that is, unwashed. (The Pharisees and all the Jews do not eat unless they give their hands a ceremonial washing, holding to the tradition of the elders).

—MARK 7:1–3 (NIV)

No matter what kind of challenges or difficulties or painful situations you go through in your life, we all have something deep within us that we can reach down and find the inner strength to get through them.

—ALANA STEWART

Dear Father God, we are truly grateful for this day. We are praying for breakthroughs in our lives. You know our challenges. Thank you for mercy and grace. Amen.

SEPTEMBER 5

Negative Forces

You bring new witnesses against me and increase your anger
toward me; your forces come against me wave upon wave.

—JOB 10:17

My family's support and the negative environment of
the day toward blacks in South Carolina became the
forces that led me out of the South—first to New York,
then to Philadelphia, where I found opportunity in the
form of a PAL gym and my trainer, Yank Durham.

—JOE FRAZIER

Father, we are so grateful for this day. We are praying to
be productive and creative—and not allow the negative
forces to hinder us. Bless us on this day. Amen.

SEPTEMBER 6

Closer Walk

"Do not come any closer," God said. "Take off your sandals,
for the place where you are standing is holy ground."
—EXODUS 3:5 (NIV)

I was baptized alongside my mother when I was eight years old.
Since then, I have tried to walk a Christian life. And now that I'm
getting older, I realized that I'm walking even closer with my God.
—ANDY GRIFFITH

Dear God, we are praying for a closer walk with you.
Bless us with your divine wisdom and knowledge. We
desire to be a blessing to you and others. Amen.

SEPTEMBER 7

Meditating

On my bed I remember you; I think of you
through the watches of the night.

—PSALM 63:6 (NIV)

During my days of deepest grief, in all of my shock,
sorrow and struggle, I sat at the feet of God. I literally
spent hours each day reading God's Word, meditating
on scripture, and praying. I intentionally spent a
significant amount of time being still before God.

—RICK WARREN

Thank you, Father, for another wake-up call. We are praying
to spend some quality time with you today, meditating on
your goodness, mercies, and grace. We love you. Amen.

SEPTEMBER 8

Change

Jesus Christ is the same yesterday and today and forever.
—HEBREWS 13:8 (NIV)

Education is the most powerful weapon which
you can use to change the world.
—NELSON MANDELA

Dear God, thank you for this day. Help us accept the things
we cannot change, the courage to change the things we
can, and the wisdom to know the difference. Amen.

SEPTEMBER 9

Disagreeable

They disagreed among themselves and began to leave after Paul
had made this final statement: "The Holy Spirit spoke the truth
to your ancestors when he said through Isaiah the prophet."

—ACTS 28:25 (NIV)

Embrace a diversity of ideas. Embrace the fact that you can
disagree with people and not be disagreeable. Embrace the
fact that you can find common ground—if you disagree
on nine out of ten things, but can find common ground
on that tenth, maybe you can make progress. If you can
find common ground, you can accomplish great things.

—DAVID BOIES

Dear Father God, thank you for this day. We are praying
to be more grateful for all our relationships. Help us learn
that we can disagree without being disagreeable. Amen.

SEPTEMBER 10

Joyful

Shout for joy to the Lord, all the earth. Worship the
Lord with gladness; come before him with joyful songs.
Know that the Lord is God. It is he who made us, and
we are his; we are his people, the sheep of his pasture.

—PSALM 100:1–3 (NIV)

Your destiny is to fulfill those things upon which you
focus most intently. So choose to keep your focus on
that which is truly magnificent, beautiful, uplifting and
joyful. your life is always moving toward something.

—RALPH MARSTON

Thank you, Father, for this day. We are grateful for
so many things. Help us be more loving, peaceful,
joyful, faithful, gentle, and kind. Amen.

Greater

You, dear children, are from God and have
overcome them, because the one who is in you is
greater than the one who is in the world.

—1 JOHN 4:4 (NIV)

The God we serve does not seek out the perfect, but
instead uses our imperfections and our shortcomings
for his greater good. I am humbled by my own
limitations. But where I am weak, He is strong.

—RICK PERRY

Dear Father God, thank you for blessing us with this new day.
We are praying for a closer walk with you. Greater is he who lives
within us than he who is in this world. Help us stay focused and
committed to your will. Put those individuals in our paths today
so that we can encourage and share the good news with. Amen.

Safety

In peace I will lie down and sleep, for you
alone, Lord, make me dwell in safety.
—PSALM 4:8 (NIV)

Home is where children find safety and security, where
we find our identities, where citizenship starts. It usually
starts with believing you're part of a community,
and that is essential to having a stable home.
—MATTHEW DESMOND

Dear Father God, we are so grateful for this day. Thank
you for watching over us as we slept last night. We are
praying for a productive week. Please guide us and
keep us safe from all harm and danger. Amen.

SEPTEMBER 13

Assignments

Then Jehoiada placed the oversight of the temple of the
Lord in the hands of the Levitical priests, to whom David
had made assignments in the temple, to present the burnt
offerings of the Lord as written in the Law of Moses,
with rejoicing and singing, as David had ordered.
—2 CHRONICLES 23:18 (NIV)

If we look upon fulfilling of assignments as building the
kingdom of God and as being an opportunity as well as a
privilege and an honor, then assignments and challenges
should certainly be given to every member of the quorum.
—JAMES E. FAUST

Dear Father, we thank you for this Friday. We are
praying for your guidance and protection on this day.
Help us stay focused on the assignments you have given
us so that we can see them to completion. Amen.

SEPTEMBER 14

Spiritual Ears

For the time will come when people will not put up with
sound doctrine. Instead, to suit their own desires, they
will gather around them a great number of teachers to say
what their itching ears want to hear. They will turn their
ears away from the truth and turn aside to myths.

—2 TIMOTHY 4:3–4 (NIV)

The relation between practical and spiritual spheres
in music is obvious, if only because it demands
ears, finger, consciousness, and intellect.

—LUCIANO BERIO

Dear God, we thank you for allowing us to hear
you when you speak to us through the Holy Spirit,
which brings all understanding. Amen.

SEPTEMBER 15

Spiritual Frequency

Dear friends, do not believe every spirit, but test the
spirits to see whether they are from God, because many
false prophets have gone out into the world.

—1 JOHN 4:1 (NIV)

Maturity is the ability to think, speak and act your feelings
within the bounds of dignity. The measure of your maturity is
how spiritual you become during the midst of your frustrations.

—SAMUEL ULLMAN

Dear Father, thank you for one more day. We are praying
to get tuned in to the right spiritual frequency, so that we
can hear you with our spiritual ears when you speak to
us. We don't want to miss out on your blessings and the
opportunity to be a blessing to someone else. Amen.

Strong Minds

Therefore, with minds that are alert and fully sober,
set your hope on the grace to be brought to you
when Jesus Christ is revealed at his coming.
—1 PETER 1:13 (NIV)

In so far as the mind is stronger than the body,
so are the ills contracted by the mind more
severe than those contracted by the body.
—MARCUS TULLIUS CICERO

Father, we pray to never take you for granted. Thank
you for giving us strong minds. We take authority over
those things that will hinder our progress today: self-
doubt, procrastination, anger, resentments, intolerance,
and lack of self-discipline and motivation. Amen.

Selfish

Do nothing out of selfish ambition or vain conceit.
Rather, in humility value others above yourselves.

—PHILIPPIANS 2:3 (NIV)

All life demands struggle. Those who have everything given to
them become lazy, selfish, and insensitive to the real values of
life. The very striving and hard work that we so constantly try
to avoid is the major building block in the person we are today.

—POPE PAUL VI

Dear Father God, thank you for this day. We pray for
your guidance and protection. Help us be less selfish and
more selfless, more loving, and less judgmental. Amen.

SEPTEMBER 18

Understanding

And the peace of God, which transcends all understanding,
will guard your hearts and your minds in Christ Jesus.
—PHILIPPIANS 4:7 (NIV)

Love is friendship that has caught fire. It is quiet
understanding, mutual confidence, sharing and forgiving. It
is loyalty through good and bad times. It settles for less than
perfection and makes allowances for human weaknesses.

—ANN LANDERS

Dear Father God, we thank you for another day. We are praying
for your help to understand our primary purposes in life so that we
don't waste precious time traveling down the wrong paths. Amen.

SEPTEMBER 19

Ordained

Aaron's sacred garments will belong to his descendants
so that they can be anointed and ordained in them.

—EXODUS 29:29 (NIV)

Marriage and family are ordained of God. The family is
the most important social unit in time and in eternity.
Under God's great plan of happiness, families can be
sealed in temples and be prepared to return to dwell
in His holy presence forever. That is eternal life!

—RUSSELL M. NELSON

Dear Father God, we thank you for this day. Help
us move closer to our destinations and the purposes
you have ordained for our lives. Amen.

SEPTEMBER 20

Watch

Watch and pray so that you will not fall into temptation.
The spirit is willing, but the flesh is weak.

—MATTHEW 26:41 (NIV)

If you want to see the true measure of a man, watch
how he treats his inferiors, not his equals.

—J. K. ROWLING

Dear God, thank you for this day. Thank you for watching over
us last night and blessing us this morning with your precious
love. Order our footsteps on this day in the directions in which
you would have us to go. Grant us your mercy and grace. Amen.

SEPTEMBER 21

Fruit of the Spirit

But the fruit of the Spirit is love, joy, peace, forbearance,
kindness, goodness, faithfulness, gentleness, and self-
control. Against such things there is no law.

—GALATIANS 5:22 (NIV)

The single dynamic that helps people be most aware of God
and most experiencing the fruit of the Spirit is gratitude.

—JOHN ORTBERG

Dear God, we are so grateful for another day. We
are praying to be more like you: more loving, kind,
patient, compassionate, and gentle. Amen.

SEPTEMBER 22

Draw

Come near to God and he will come near to you. Wash your
hands, you sinners, and purify your hearts, you double-minded.
—JAMES 4:8 (NIV)

No books ever go into my laboratory. The thing I am
to do and the way are revealed to me the moment I am
inspired to create something new. Without God to draw
aside the curtain, I would be helpless. Only alone can I
draw close enough to God to discover His secrets.

— GEORGE WASHINGTON CARVER

Dear God, how great thou art. We love and adore you. We are
praying on this day that you will draw us closer to you. Amen.

SEPTEMBER 23

Creator

But Abram said to the king of Sodom, "With
raised hand I have sworn an oath to the Lord, God
Most High, Creator of heaven and earth."
—GENESIS 14:22 (NIV)

In my deepest, darkest moments, what really got me through was
a prayer. Sometimes my prayer was "Help me." Sometimes a prayer
was "Thank you." What I've discovered is that intimate connection
and communication with my creator will always get me through
because I know my support, my help, is just a prayer away.
—IYANLA VANZANT

Dear Creator of the heavens and earth, we come before thee on
this day as humble as we can be, asking for your forgiveness of all
our sins. Help us be better and more pleasing in your sight. Amen.

SEPTEMBER 24

Increases

Do not be overawed when others grow rich, when
the splendor of their houses increases.
—PSALM 49:16 (NIV)

Becoming a father increases your capacity for love and your
level of patience. It opens up another door in a person—a door
which you may not even have known was there. That's what
I feel with my son. There's suddenly another level of love that
expands. My son is my greatest joy, out of everything in my life.
—KYLE MACLACHLAN

Dear gracious Father, thank you for this day. We are
praying for increases on this day. We are asking for
financial blessings. You said in your Word that we
should have life and a life of abundance. Amen.

SEPTEMBER 25

Relationships

In your relationships with one another, have
the same mind-set as Christ Jesus.
—PHILIPPIANS 2:5 (NIV)

When we understand the connection between how we live
and how long we live, it's easier to make different choices.
Instead of viewing the time we spend with friends and family
as luxuries, we can see that these relationships are among the
most powerful determinants of our well-being and survival.
—DEAN ORNISH

Dear God, we thank you for another day. We are praying
for our families, friends, coworkers, and associates on
this day. Enrich our relationships, keep them strong,
and build them up where they are weak. Amen.

SEPTEMBER 26

Grateful

Sing to the Lord with grateful praise; make
music to our God on the harp.
—PSALM 147:7 (NIV)

Be grateful for what you have and stop complaining—it bores
everybody else, does you no good, and doesn't solve any problems.
—ZIG ZIGLAR

Dear God, we are so grateful for one more day among
the living on this side of the sky. We are praying to
more grateful and thankful for life. Amen.

SEPTEMBER 27

Pleased

If the Lord is pleased with us, he will lead us into that land,
a land flowing with milk and honey, and will give it to us.
—NUMBERS 14:8 (NIV)

In almost everything that touches our everyday life on earth,
God is pleased when we're pleased. He wills that we be as free
as birds to soar and sing our maker's praise without anxiety.
— AIDEN WILSON TOZER

Dear God, we are so pleased that you blessed us with
another day. We are praying to be our very best on this
day and not take your grace for granted. Amen.

Distractions

I am saying this for your own good, not to restrict you, but that
you may live in a right way in undivided devotion to the Lord.
—1 CORINTHIANS 7:35 (NIV)

Whatever you want to do, do with full passion and
work really hard towards it. Don't look anywhere else.
There will be a few distractions, but if you can be
true to yourself, you will be successful for sure.
—VIRAT KOHLI

Dear God, thank you for one more day. We are praying
to keep focus on the things that really matter and not get
distracted by the things that short-circuit our goals. Amen.

SEPTEMBER 29

Strength

He gives strength to the weary and
increases the power of the weak.
—ISAIAH 40:29 (NIV)

Every great dream begins with a dreamer. Always remember,
you have within you the strength, the patience, and the
passion to reach for the stars to change the world.
—HARRIET TUBMAN

Dear God, one more day in you grace. On this
day, help us talk in faith. We can do all things
through Christ who strengthens us. Amen.

SEPTEMBER 30

Trials and Tribulations

I have told you these things, so that in me you may
have peace. In this world you will have trouble.
But take heart! I have overcome the world.

—JOHN 16:33 (NIV)

We all face storms in life. Some are more difficult
than others, but we all go through trials and
tribulation. That's why we have the gift of faith.

—JOYCE MEYER

Dear God, we are thankful for this day and the ending of
this month. Thank you for being with us as we went through
trials and tribulations. We pray for a better October. Amen.

OCTOBER 1

Safety

In peace I will lie down and sleep, for you
alone, Lord, make me dwell in safety.
Psalm 4:8 (NIV)
We shall listen, not lecture; learn, not threaten. We will enhance
our safety by earning the respect of others and showing respect
for them. In short, our foreign policy will rest on the traditional
American values of restraint and empathy, not on military might.
—THEODORE C. SORENSEN

Father, we are praying for the safety of our children
on this day. Please keep them safe from all harm
and danger. In the name of Jesus. Amen.

OCTOBER 2

Self-Confidence

When all our enemies heard about this, all the surrounding
nations were afraid and lost their self-confidence, because they
realized that this work had been done with the help of our God.

—NEHEMIAH 6:16 (NIV)

Self-esteem should not be confused with self-confidence. Self-
confidence is believing in your competence and your ability to do
something, whereas self-esteem is believing in your goodness.

—MARK GOULSTON

Heavenly Father, we thank you for this day. Help
us with self-confidence as we strive to be our very
best today. In the name of Jesus. Amen.

OCTOBER 3

Health

Nevertheless, I will bring health and healing to it; I will heal my people and will let them enjoy abundant peace and security.

—JEREMIAH 33:6 (NIV)

You can look in the mirror and find a million things wrong with yourself. Or you can look in the mirror and think, *I feel good, I have my health, and I'm so blessed.* That's the way I choose to look at it.

—ISLA FISHER

Dear Father, we thank you for another week. We pray that we will make healthier choices: mentally, physically, and spiritually. In the name of Jesus. Amen.

OCTOBER 4

Mental

Those who live according to the flesh have their minds set
on what the flesh desires; but those who live in accordance
with the Spirit have their minds set on what the Spirit
desires. The mind governed by the flesh is death, but
the mind governed by the Spirit is life and peace.

—ROMANS 8:5–6 (NIV)

Nothing can stop the man with the right mental
attitude from achieving his goal; nothing on earth can
help the man with the wrong mental attitude.

—THOMAS JEFFERSON

Dear Father, thank you for this day. We are praying for
positive mental attitudes. Help us focus on the things
that matter most. In the name of Jesus. Amen.

OCTOBER 5

Challenge

Now the Ephraimites asked Gideon, "Why have you treated
us like this? Why didn't you call us when you went to
fight Midian?" And they challenged him vigorously.

—JUDGES 8:1 (NIV)

You should never view your challenges as a disadvantage.
Instead, it's important for you to understand that
your experience facing and overcoming adversity
is actually one of your biggest advantages.

—MICHELLE OBAMA

Father, we thank you for this Thursday. Give us
strength to press forward during times of challenges.
The blessings are in the pressing. INJ. Amen.

OCTOBER 6

Anxiety

Cast all your anxiety on him because he cares for you.
—1 PETER 5:7 (NIV)

Religion is meant to teach us true spiritual human
character. It is meant for self-transformation. It is
meant to transform anxiety into peace, arrogance into
humility, envy into compassion, to awaken the pure soul
in man and his love for the Source, which is God.
—RADHANATH SWAMI

Father, we sincerely thank you for this day. We come
against fear, anxiety, and procrastination. We can do all
things through Christ who strengthened us. Amen.

OCTOBER 7

Progress

The evening meal was in progress, and the devil had
already prompted Judas, the son of Simon Iscariot, to
betray Jesus. Jesus knew that the Father had put all things
under his power, and that he had come from God and was
returning to God; so he got up from the meal, took off his
outer clothing, and wrapped a towel around his waist.

—JOHN 13:2–17 (NIV)

Coming together is a beginning; keeping together
is progress; working together is success.

—EDWARD EVERETT HALE

Father, thank you for this day. We are praying for self-
discipline and the power to rise above any situations that will
hinder our progress today. In the name of Jesus. Amen.

OCTOBER 8

Productive

Again, it will be like a man going on a journey, who called
his servants and entrusted his wealth to them. To one he
gave five bags of gold, to another two bags, and to another
one bag, each according to his ability. Then he went on his
journey. The man who had received five bags of gold went at
once and put his money to work and gained five bags more.

—MATTHEW 25:14–30 (NIV)

The more generous we are, the more joyous we become. The
more cooperative we are, the more valuable we become. The
more enthusiastic we are, the more productive we become.
The more serving we are, the more prosperous we become.

—WILLIAM ARTHUR WARD

Dear Father, we thank you for this day. We are
praying for a productive week. Please help us stay
focused. In the name of Jesus, we pray. Amen.

OCTOBER 9

Protection

Whoever dwells in the shelter of the Most High will rest in the shadow of the Almighty. I will say of the Lord, "He is my refuge and my fortress, my God, in whom I trust." Surely he will save you from the fowler's snare and from the deadly pestilence.

—PSALM 91:1–3 (NIV)

Confidence ... thrives on honesty, on honor, on the sacredness of obligations, on faithful protection and on unselfish performance. Without them it cannot live.

—FRANKLIN D. ROOSEVELT

Dear Father, thank you for your love and protection throughout this week. Guide us into reaching out to someone today who needs to be encouraged. Amen.

OCTOBER 10

Motivation

And let us consider how we may spur one
another on toward love and good deeds.

—HEBREWS 10:24 (NIV)

Desire is the key to motivation, but it's determination
and commitment to an unrelenting pursuit of your
goal—a commitment to excellence—that will
enable you to attain the success you seek.

—MARIO ANDRETTI

Father, we thank you for our gifts and talents. We are
praying for motivation and determination to be all that
you have created us to be. In the name of Jesus. Amen.

OCTOBER 11

Our Needs

Our people must learn to devote themselves to
doing what is good, in order to provide for urgent
needs and not live unproductive lives.

—TITUS 3:14 (NIV)

Giving frees us from the familiar territory of our
own needs by opening our mind to the unexplained
worlds occupied by the needs of others.

—BARBARA BUSH

Dear Father God, we are praying for breakthroughs
today. You know exactly what we need. We surrender all
to you. In the name of Jesus Christ, we pray. Amen.

Be Our Best

Our days may come to seventy years, or eighty, if our
strength endures; yet the best of them are but trouble
and sorrow, for they quickly pass, and we fly away.

—PSALM 90:10

Marriage can be a magnificent lesson in
becoming our best selves; that is true.

—MARIANNE WILLIAMSON

Dear God, we humble ourselves before you. Help
us be the very best we can be. Guide and direct us
throughout this day. In the name of Jesus. Amen.

OCTOBER 13

Take for Granted

Adam made love to his wife again, and she gave birth to
a son and named him Seth, saying, "God has granted me
another child in place of Abel, since Cain killed him."

—GENESIS 4:25 (NIV)

The more often we see the things around us—even the beautiful
and wonderful things—the more they become invisible to us.
That is why we often take for granted the beauty of this world:
the flowers, the trees, the birds, the clouds—even those we love.
Because we see things so often, we see them less and less.

—JOSEPH B. WIRTHLIN

Dear Father, we are grateful for this day. We pray that we
never take your love, mercy, and grace for granted. Give us
this day our daily bread. In the name of Jesus. Amen.

Power

Abraham will surely become a great and powerful nation,
and all nations on earth will be blessed through him.
—GENESIS 18:18 (NIV)

Knowledge is power. Information is liberating. Education is
the premise of progress, in every society, in every family.

—KOFI ANNAN

Dear Father, we are not asking for tasks equal to our powers,
but for your power, which is greater than any task. We can
do all things with your help. In the name of Jesus. Amen.

OCTOBER 15

Concentration

Finally, brothers and sisters, whatever is true, whatever
is noble, whatever is right, whatever is pure, whatever is
lovely, whatever is admirable—if anything is excellent
or praiseworthy—think about such things.

—PHILIPPIANS 4:8 (NIV)

Elegance is achieved when all that is superfluous
has been discarded and the human being discovers
simplicity and concentration: the simpler and more
sober the posture, the more beautiful it will be.

—PAULO COELHO

Dear Father God, we need your help to improve
our concentration on this day to complete the tasks
before us. In the name of Jesus, we pray. Amen.

OCTOBER 16

Confidence

So do not throw away your confidence; it will be richly rewarded.
—HEBREWS 10:35 (NIV)

Everyone has attitude, and I think everyone should have attitude.
But I know I have attitude, but that's just, I think if you don't
have attitude, it comes only with self-confidence. So if you don't
have self-confidence, you won't have attitude, and I think there's a
difference when you have attitude and when you have arrogance.

—SANIA MIRZA

Dear Father, we are praying to walk in confidence, not
allowing ourselves to be distracted from our primary
purpose in life. In the name of Jesus, we do pray. Amen.

OCTOBER 17

Unbelief

Immediately the boy's father exclaimed, "I do
believe; help me overcome my unbelief!"
—MARK 9:24 (NIV)

No man is excluded from calling upon God, the gate of salvation
is set open unto all men: neither is there any other thing which
keepeth us back from entering in, save only our own unbelief.
—JOHN CALVIN

Dear Father God, we are grateful for this day. Help us
with our unbelief. We are praying for our faith in you
to increase. In the name of Jesus, we pray. Amen.

OCTOBER 18

Awareness

Aware of their discussion, Jesus asked them: "Why are
you talking about having no bread? Do you still not see or
understand? Are your hearts hardened? Do you have eyes but
fail to see, and ears but fail to hear? And don't you remember?"
—MARK 8:17–18 (NIV)

Whatever we are waiting for—peace of mind, contentment,
grace, the inner awareness of simple abundance—
it will surely come to us, but only when we are ready
to receive it with an open and grateful heart.
—SARAH BAN BREATHNACH

Father, we are praying for awareness and power to
move to that next level in our lives. Grant us deeper
understandings. In the name of Jesus, we pray. Amen.

OCTOBER 19

Power of Prayer

Is anyone among you in trouble? Let them pray. Is anyone
happy? Let them sing songs of praise. Is anyone among you
sick? Let them call the elders of the church to pray over them
and anoint them with oil in the name of the Lord. And the
prayer offered in faith will make the sick person well; the Lord
will raise them up. If they have sinned, they will be forgiven.

—JAMES 5:13–18 (NIV)

I've always believed in the power of prayer. One prayer
can accomplish more than a thousand plans. That
isn't a magic formula, but it's an idea that if you pray,
keep praying and then praying some more.

—MARK BATTERSON

Dear Father, thank you for the power of prayer. Help us
fully understand the power of the tongue—what we speak
is what we get. In the name of Jesus, we pray. Amen.

Deliverance

But God sent me ahead of you to preserve for you a remnant
on earth and to save your lives by a great deliverance.

—GENESIS 45:7 (NIV)

The more I am in a position to be tried in faith with reference
to my body, my family, my service for the Lord, my business,
etc., the more shall I have opportunity of seeing God's help
and deliverance; and every fresh instance, in which He helps
and delivers me, will tend towards the increase of my faith.

—GEORGE MULLER

Dear Father, we thank you for deliverance. We pray that we
will move forward and stop looking back to the past, reliving
the pain in our minds. In the name of Jesus, we pray. Amen.

OCTOBER 21

Gentleness

By the humility and gentleness of Christ, I appeal
to you—I, Paul, who am "timid" when face to face
with you, but "bold" toward you when away!
—2 CORINTHIANS 10:1 (NIV)

A Christian reveals true humility by showing the gentleness
of Christ, by being always ready to help others, by speaking
kind words and performing unselfish acts, which elevate and
ennoble the most sacred message that has come to our world.
—ELLEN G. WHITE

Dear Father, we are praying for peace, love, joy
happiness, gentleness, forbearance, and patience.
In the name of Jesus, we pray. Amen.

OCTOBER 22

Spiritual Growth

For this reason I kneel before the Father, from whom
every family in heaven and on earth derives its name. I
pray that out of his glorious riches he may strengthen you
with power through his Spirit in your inner being.
—EPHESIANS 3:14–21 (NIV)

A spiritual partnership is a partnership between equals
for the purpose of spiritual growth. Spiritual partners use
their delightful experiences together as well as their power
struggles to learn about themselves and change themselves.
—GARY ZUKAV

Dear Father, we are praying for spiritual growth. Show
us your purpose for our lives and grant us the power to
move forward. In the name of Jesus, we pray. Amen.

OCTOBER 23

Enslaved

Don't you know that when you offer yourselves to
someone as obedient slaves, you are slaves of the one
you obey—whether you are slaves to sin, which leads to
death, or to obedience, which leads to righteousness?
—ROMANS 6:16 (NIV)

We are shallow because we have become enslaved
by gross materialism, the glitter of gold and its
equivalents, for which reason we think that only the
material goods of this earth can satisfy us and we must
therefore grab as much as can while we are able.
—F. SIONIL JOSE

Dear Father God, we are praying to be separated from
the things that keep us enslaved and unproductive in
our lives. In the name of Jesus, we pray. Amen.

OCTOBER 24

God's Love

But I am like an olive tree flourishing in the house of
God; I trust in God's unfailing love for ever and ever.
—PSALM 52:8 (NIV)

I know God loves me. I tell people all the time I'm one of
his favorite childs. I had to believe in something bigger than
me—bigger than man. I had to believe that God would
send somebody across my path to keep my dreams alive.
—DARLENE LOVE

Dear Father God, thank you for another day in your
grace. We are so grateful for everlasting love. Please
help us love our neighbors—as you love us. Amen.

OCTOBER 25

Our Provider

Command those who are rich in this present world not
to be arrogant nor to put their hope in wealth, which is
so uncertain, but to put their hope in God, who richly
provides us with everything for our enjoyment.

—1 TIMOTHY 6:17 (NIV)

I believe if you keep your faith, you keep your trust, you keep the
right attitude, if you're grateful, you'll see God open up new doors.

—JOEL OSTEEN

Dear Father God, we thank you for another day. Thank
you for being our provider and for giving us shelter, food,
clothes, and a reasonable portion of health. Amen.

OCTOBER 26

Broken Hearts

He heals the brokenhearted and binds up their wounds.
—PSALM 147:3 (NIV)

Paris is the destination for brokenhearted American
women. I think men go there and have their hearts broken,
but women come there with their hearts broken.
—WHIT STILLMAN

Dear God, we are so grateful for this day. We are praying
today for those who are lonely and brokenhearted. Please
help them and mend their brokenness. Amen.

OCTOBER 27

Right Decisions

For day after day they seek me out; they seem eager to know
my ways, as if they were a nation that does what is right and
has not forsaken the commands of its God. They ask me for
just decisions and seem eager for God to come near them.

—ISAIAH 58:2 (NIV)

It's about having an active lifestyle, staying healthy, and making
the right decisions. Life is about balance. Not everybody wants
to run a marathon, but we could all start working out and being
active, whether you walk to work or take an extra flight of stairs.

—APOLO OHNO

Dear God, thank you for another day that we have not
seen before and will not see again. We are praying to be
the very best we can be on this day. Help us make the right
decisions and yield to your will and not our own. Amen.

OCTOBER 28

God's Joy

So that I may come to you with joy, by God's
will, and in your company be refreshed.

—ROMANS 15:32 (NIV)

All true happiness, pure joy, sweet bounties, and
untroubled pleasure lie in knowledge of God and
love of God; they cannot exist without them.

—SAID NURSI

Dear Father, this is the day that you have made, and we will rejoice
and be glad in it. We are praying for your joy in our lives, Father,
so that we can live life to its fullest with everlasting joy. Amen.

OCTOBER 29

Strong and Powerful

Yet even angels, although they are stronger and more
powerful, do not heap abuse on such beings when
bringing judgment on them from the Lord.
—2 PETER 2:11 (NIV)

Instead of focusing on that circumstances that you
cannot change—focus strongly and powerfully
on the circumstances that you can.
—JOY PAGE

Dear God, Creator of the heavens and earth, we humble ourselves
before you on this day. You have all power in your hands.
Help us be strong and focused throughout this day. Amen.

OCTOBER 30

Empower

When Jesus had called the Twelve together, he gave them power
and authority to drive out all demons and to cure diseases,
and he sent them out to proclaim the kingdom of God and to
heal the sick. He told them: "Take nothing for the journey—
no staff, no bag, no bread, no money, no extra shirt."

—LUKE 9:1–6 (NIV)

Confidence and empowerment are cousins in my opinion.
Empowerment comes from within and typically it's
stemmed and fostered by self-assurance. To feel empowered
is to feel free and that's when people do their best
work. You can't fake confidence or empowerment.

—AMY JO MARTIN

Dear God, we thank you for this day. Please help
us with our unbelief and empower us with your
truth, understanding, and wisdom. Amen.

OCTOBER 31

Acknowledge God

Acknowledge and take to heart this day that the Lord is God
in heaven above and on the earth below. There is no other.
—DEUTERONOMY 4:39 (NIV)

God had brought me to my knees and made me
acknowledge my own nothingness, and out of that
knowledge I had been reborn. I was no longer the center
of my life and therefore I could see God in everything.
—BEDE GRIFFITHS

Dear God, we thank you for this day. We acknowledge
that we cannot do anything but fail without you. Thank
you for never leaving us or forsaking us. Amen.

NOVEMBER 1

Worthless

The seven lean, ugly cows that came up afterward are seven
years, and so are the seven worthless heads of grain scorched
by the east wind: They are seven years of famine.

—GENESIS 41:27 (NIV)

Because of lack of moral principle, human life becomes
worthless. Moral principle, truthfulness, is a key
factor. If we lose that, then there is no future.

—DALAI LAMA

Dear God, give us the courage to separate ourselves from dead
weight. Those things are worthless and keep us stuck. Amen.

NOVEMBER 2

Gift of Life

For the wages of sin is death, but the gift of God
is eternal life in Christ Jesus our Lord.

—ROMANS 6:23 (NIV)

God gave us the gift of life in heaven. Many people are given this
gift, but they never open it. They never do anything with it.

—RICK WARREN

Dear God, we thank you for the gift of life. We pray that we do
not to waste it on things that are not creative or productive. Amen.

NOVEMBER 3

Grace and Mercy

Grace, mercy, and peace from God the Father and from Jesus
Christ, the Father's Son, will be with us in truth and love.

—2 JOHN 3 (NIV)

God's mercy and grace give me hope—
for myself, and for our world.

—BILLY GRAHAM

Dear God, thank you for this day. We never want to take you for
granted. Thank you for your grace and mercy each day. Amen.

NOVEMBER 4

Procrastination

A sluggard's appetite is never filled, but the
desires of the diligent are fully satisfied.

—PROVERBS 13:4 (NIV)

Procrastination is the bad habit of putting off until the day after
tomorrow what should have been done the day before yesterday.

—NAPOLEON HILL

Dear Father, we are so grateful for this day. We are praying to be
better than yesterday. Help us with our procrastination. Amen.

NOVEMBER 5

Distraction

Fixing our eyes on Jesus, the Pioneer and Perfecter of faith.
For the joy set before him he endured the cross, scorning its
shame, and sat down at the right hand of the throne of God.

—HEBREWS 12:2 (NIV)

Successful people maintain a positive focus in life no matter what
is going on around them. They stay focused on their past successes
rather than their past failures, and on the next action steps they
need to take to get them closer to the fulfillment of their goals
rather than all the other distractions that life presents to them.

—JACK CANFIELD

Dear Father, we thank you for this day. Help us stay focused
and not be distracted by people, places, and things. Amen.

Disappointments

"Has not my hand made all these things, and so they came into being?" declares the Lord. "These are the ones I look on with favor: those who are humble and contrite in spirit, and who tremble at my word."

—ISAIAH 66:2 (NIV)

It's easy to get negative because you get beat down. You go through a few disappointments and it's easy to stay in that negative frame of mind. Choosing to be positive and having a grateful attitude is a whole cliché, but your attitude is going to determine how you're going to live your life.

—JOEL OSTEEN

Dear Father, we are praying to get over all past hurts, pains, and disappointments. Grant us the fullness of life. Amen.

Gifts and Talents

Again, it will be like a man going on a journey, who called
his servants and entrusted his wealth to them. To one he
gave five bags of gold, to another two bags, and to another
one bag, each according to his ability. Then he went on his
journey. The man who had received five bags of gold went at
once and put his money to work and gained five bags more.

—MATTHEW 25:14–30 (NIV)

I think one of the keys to leadership is recognizing that
everybody has gifts and talents. A good leader will learn
how to harness those gifts toward the same goal.

—BEN CARSON

Dear God, we thank you for our individual gifts
and talents. Help us use them wisely. Amen.

NOVEMBER 8

Blessings from God

Every good and perfect gift is from above, coming
down from the Father of the heavenly lights, who
does not change like shifting shadows.

—JAMES 1:17 (NIV)

However many blessings we expect from God, His infinite
liberality will always exceed all our wishes and our thoughts.

—JOHN CALVIN

Thank you, God, for the blessings you have given us. We
can get what we don't have with what we do have. Amen.

Patience

A person's wisdom yields patience; it is to
one's glory to overlook an offense.

—PROVERBS 19:11 (NIV)

Every great dream begins with a dreamer. Always remember,
you have within you the strength, the patience, and the
passion to reach for the stars to change the world.

—HARRIET TUBMAN

Dear God, thank you for your patience. We have all fallen short
in one way or another, but you continue to love us. Amen.

NOVEMBER 10

Eternal Purposes

According to his eternal purpose that he
accomplished in Christ Jesus our Lord.
—EPHESIANS 3:11 (NIV)

Providence has nothing good or high in store for one
who does not resolutely aim at something high or good.
A purpose is the eternal condition of success.
—THORNTON WILDER

Dear Father God, we thank you for all things—big and small.
Please direct us in the direction in which you would have us
go to complete your eternal purposes for our lives. Amen.

NOVEMBER 11

Our Purpose

See what great love the Father has lavished on us, that we should be called children of God! And that is what we are! The reason the world does not know us is that it did not know him. Dear friends, now we are children of God, and what we will be has not yet been made known. But we know that when Christ appears, we shall be like him, for we shall see him as he is. All who have this hope in him purify themselves, just as he is pure.

—1 JOHN 3:1–3 (NIV)

When our purpose is external, we may never find it. If we tie our purpose or meaning to our vocation, goal, or an activity, we're more than likely setting ourselves up for suffering down the line.

—KRIS CARR

Dear God, we are grateful for this day. Help us stay focused on our purpose and meaningful things. Amen.

God Centered

And God said, "This is the sign of the covenant I am making between me and you and every living creature with you, a covenant for all generations to come."

—GENESIS 9:12 (NIV)

The problem is that God is being dismissed from the culture, and that vacuum is allowing, or is the basis for, the deterioration of society. That is because Christians have not kept Him in the center of the culture.

—TONY EVANS

Dear Father, we are so grateful for this day. We are praying to keep our focus on you and allow you to guide us throughout this day. Amen.

NOVEMBER 13

Soft Whispers

For my yoke is easy and my burden is light.
—MATTHEW 11:30 (NIV)

Just as in earthly life lovers long for the moment when they
are able to breathe forth their love for each other, to let their
souls blend in a soft whisper, so the mystic longs for the
moment when in prayer he can, as it were, creep into God.
—SOREN KIERKEGAARD

Dear Father God, we are praying to be centered with you on this
day. As you speak in soft whispers, we can hear your voice. Amen.

Release All Worries

Cast all your anxiety on him because he cares for you.
—1 PETER 5:7 (NIV)

Even though you may want to move forward in your life, you may
have one foot on the brakes. In order to be free, we must learn how
to let go. Release the hurt. Release the fear. Refuse to entertain
your old pain. The energy it takes to hang onto the past is holding
you back from a new life. What is it you would let go of today?
—MARY MANIN MORRISSEY

Dear Father, we are praying to release all worries
and fears to you. In the name of Jesus. Amen.

Wise Decisions

Trust in the Lord with all your heart and lean not
on your own understanding; in all your ways submit
to him, and he will make your paths straight.

—PROVERBS 3:5–6 (NIV)

The wise use of your freedom to make your own decisions
is crucial to your spiritual growth, now and for eternity.

—RUSSELL M. NELSON

Dear Father God, we are grateful for this day. We pray to make
wise decisions and be productive. In the name of Jesus. Amen.

NOVEMBER 16

Distractions

I am saying this for your own good, not to restrict you, but that you may live in a right way in undivided devotion to the Lord.
—1 CORINTHIANS 7:35 (NIV)

Whatever you want to do, do with full passion and work really hard towards it. Don't look anywhere else. There will be a few distractions, but if you can be true to yourself, you will be successful for sure.
—VIRAT KOHLI

Dear Father, we are praying to know our purposes— so we don't get distracted by things that are not for us. In the name of Jesus. Amen.

Ordained

Your eyes saw my unformed body; all the days ordained for me
were written in your book before one of them came to be.

—PSALM 139:16 (NIV)

Marriage and family are ordained of God. The family is
the most important social unit in time and in eternity.
Under God's great plan of happiness, families can be
sealed in temples and be prepared to return to dwell
in His holy presence forever. That is eternal life!

—RUSSELL M. NELSON

Dear God, help us leave behind procrastination
and charge forward into the future you've ordained
for us. In the name of Jesus. Amen.

NOVEMBER 18

Financial Blessings

And constant friction between people of corrupt
mind, who have been robbed of the truth and who
think that godliness is a means to financial gain.
—1 TIMOTHY 6:5 (NIV)

If you want to reap financial blessings, you have to sow financially.
—JOEL OSTEEN

Dear God, you said in your Word, 'We have not, because
we ask not.' We are asking today for financial, health, and
relationship blessings. In the name of Jesus. Amen.

NOVEMBER 19

Positive People

Finally, brothers and sisters, whatever is true, whatever
is noble, whatever is right, whatever is pure, whatever is
lovely, whatever is admirable—if anything is excellent
or praiseworthy—think about such things.

—PHILIPPIANS 4:8 (NIV)

When you think positively, you attract positive people. If I'm on a
mission to be successful, and I'm positive all the time, then more
positive people will come around me, and we'll help each other. If
you're negative, you'll find yourself surrounded by negative people.

—ASTRO

Dear God, we are praying for your help to connect with
positive and productive people rather than those who
drain our energy. In the name of Jesus. Amen.

New Mercies

Because of the Lord's great love we are not consumed,
for his compassions never fail. They are new
every morning; great is your faithfulness.

—LAMENTATIONS 3:22–23 (NIV)

God's mercy is fresh and new every morning.

—JOYCE MEYER

Dear Father, we thank you for this Monday. Help
us make healthy choices today. Thank you for
new mercies. In the name of Jesus. Amen.

NOVEMBER 21

God's Power

With great power the apostles continued to testify
to the resurrection of the Lord Jesus. And God's
grace was so powerfully at work in them all.

—ACTS 4:33 (NIV)

We are under God's power, and we can do
nothing but by the power of God, and woe shall
hereafter be to us if we abuse this power.

—JOHN WYCLIFFE

Dear God, we are grateful for this day. Help us
utilize the power you have given us and walk in
your authority. In the name of Jesus. Amen.

NOVEMBER 22

Disobedience to God

Just as you who were at one time disobedient to God have
now received mercy as a result of their disobedience.

—ROMANS 11:30 (NIV)

You see, rebellion, and the disobedience it causes, keeps us from
having the power of God that's available to us as Christians.

—JOYCE MEYER

Dear God, we pray to look past the opportunities for disobedience
and toward your marvelous light. In the name of Jesus. Amen.

NOVEMBER 23

Gift of Life

For the wages of sin is death, but the gift of God
is eternal life in Christ Jesus our Lord.
—ROMANS 6:23 (NIV)

God gave us the gift of life in heaven. Many people are given this
gift, but they never open it. They never do anything with it.
—RICK WARREN

Dear God, we are so grateful for another day among
the living. We are praying to never take this gift of
life for granted. Bless us on this day. Amen.

Grace and Mercy

Grace, mercy, and peace from God the Father and from Jesus
Christ, the Father's Son, will be with us in truth and love.

—2 JOHN 3:1 (NIV)

God's mercy and grace give me hope—
for myself, and for our world.

—BILLY GRAHAM

Dear Father God, we thank you for new grace and
mercies each and every day. We pray to never take your
kindness for granted. Thank you for all things. Amen.

NOVEMBER 25

Protection and Covering

But let all who take refuge in you be glad; let them ever
sing for joy. Spread your protection over them, that
those who love your name may rejoice in you.

—PSALM 5:11 (NIV)

May the perfect grace and eternal love of Christ our
Lord be our never-failing protection and help.

—SAINT IGNATIUS

Dear God, thank you for another day you have prepared
for us. We are praying for your protection and covering
on this day. Bless our families and loved ones. Amen.

Blessing to Others

Surely you have granted him unending blessings and
made him glad with the joy of your presence.

—PSALM 21:6 (NIV)

God offers us counsel not just for our own safety, but for the
safety of His other children, whom we should love. There are few
comforts so sweet as to know that we have been an instrument in
the hands of God in leading someone else to safety. That blessing
generally requires the faith to follow counsel when it is hard to do.

—HENRY B. EYRING

Dear gracious Father, we thank you for this day our daily
bread. We are praying to be faithful to you on this day and to
be the very best we can be to ourselves and others. Amen.

NOVEMBER 27

Negative Energy

For fools speak folly, their hearts are bent on evil: They practice
ungodliness and spread error concerning the Lord; the hungry
they leave empty and from the thirsty they withhold water.

—ISAIAH 32:6 (NIV)

I realized that if my thoughts immediately affect my body, I
should be careful about what I think. Now if I get angry, I ask
myself why I feel that way. If I can find the source of my anger,
I can turn that negative energy into something positive.

—YOKO ONO

Dear God, we thank you again for waking us this
morning and giving us this day. We are praying to be
focused and productive. Help us stay away from the
negative energies that will distract us. Amen.

Adoration

Yours, Lord, is the greatness and the power and the glory
and the majesty and the splendor, for everything in heaven
and earth is yours. yours, Lord, is the kingdom; you are
exalted as head over all. Wealth and honor come from you;
you are the ruler of all things. In your hands are strength
and power to exalt and give strength to all. Now, our God,
we give you thanks, and praise your glorious name.

—1 CHRONICLES 29:11–14 (NIV)

Christmas in Bethlehem. The ancient dream: a cold, clear
night made brilliant by a glorious star, the smell of incense,
shepherds and wise men falling to their knees in adoration
of the sweet baby, the incarnation of perfect love.

—LUCINDA FRANKS

Dear God, we want to take the time to say thank
you for all things—big and small. Thank you for
your tender loving care. Thank you for your healing
power. We love you and adore you. Amen.

Holy Spirit

But the Advocate, the Holy Spirit, whom the Father
will send in my name, will teach you all things and
will remind you of everything I have said to you.
—JOHN 14:26 (NIV)

God will never direct us to be prideful, arrogant,
and unforgiving, immoral or slothful or full of fear.
We step into these things because we are insensitive
to the leadership of the Holy Spirit within us.
—CHARLES STANLEY

Dear God, we thank you for this day. We are
praying to be closer to you on this day. Thank you
for your Spirit, which lives within us. Amen.

NOVEMBER 30

God's Kingdom

All this is evidence that God's judgment is right,
and as a result you will be counted worthy of the
kingdom of God, for which you are suffering.

—2 THESSALONIANS 1:5 (NIV)

What God wants is for us to live by His rules, resulting in the
receiving of His blessing and power. When we as Christians,
celebrating our differences, join together as the house of
God representing the kingdom of God for the glory of God,
we get the response of God to our presence in history.

—TONY EVANS

Dear Father, we thank you for the gift of eternal
life. We are praying that we will stay focused
on building your kingdom. Amen.

DECEMBER 1

Gift of Life

For the wages of sin is death, but the gift of God
is eternal life in Christ Jesus our Lord.
—ROMANS 6:23 (NIV)

God gave us the gift of life in heaven. Many people are given this
gift, but they never open it. They never do anything with it.
—RICK WARREN

Thank you, Father, for the gift of life. We pray
that we never take it for granted. Amen.

DECEMBER 2

Opening Doors

Yet he gave a command to the skies above
and opened the doors of the heavens.

—PSALM 78:23 (NIV)

Temptation is the devil looking through the keyhole.
Yielding is opening the door and inviting him in.

—BILLY SUNDAY

Thank you, Father, for opening doors that no human can
close and closing doors that no human can open. Amen.

DECEMBER 3

Good Health

Dear friend, I pray that you may enjoy good health and that all may go well with you, even as your soul is getting along well.

—3 JOHN 1:2

My trust in God flows out of the experience of his loving me, day in and day out, whether the day is stormy or fair, whether I'm sick or in good health, whether I'm in a state of grace or disgrace. He comes to me where I live and loves me as I am.

—BRENNAN MANNING

Dear Father, we thank you for good health. We are praying for all who are sick—and we add a special prayer for the elderly. Amen.

DECEMBER 4

God, Our Provider

Lord our God, all this abundance that we have provided
for building you a temple for your Holy Name comes
from your hand, and all of it belongs to you.
—1 CHRONICLES 29:16 (NIV)

I believe if you keep your faith, you keep your trust, you keep the
right attitude, if you're grateful, you'll see God open up new doors.
—JOEL OSTEEN

Father, we thank you for providing for all our needs and more.
We are praying for blessings on the less fortunate. Amen.

DECEMBER 5

Proper Balance

The boundary lines have fallen for me in pleasant places; surely I have a delightful inheritance.

—PSALM 16:6 (NIV)

In order to be totally spontaneous, you can't be too obsessed with accuracy, but if you're inaccurate in a drawing, it will look fake, and when you act, it will sound fake. You have to find miraculously some proper balance between the two, but there's no formula.

—PETER FALK

Dear God, we thank you for this day. We are praying to find the proper balance in our lives so we can be more productive. Amen.

DECEMBER 6

Freedom of Choice

So Gad went to David and said to him, "This is
what the Lord says: 'Take your choice.'"

—1 CHRONICLES 21:11 (NIV)

I have no choice about whether or not I have Parkinson's.
I have nothing but choices about how I react to it. In
those choices, there's freedom to do a lot of things in
areas that I wouldn't have otherwise found myself in.

—MICHAEL J. FOX

Dear Father, we thank you for the freedom of choice. Amen.

DECEMBER 7

Reasonable

Just as Paul was about to speak, Gallio said to them, "If you
Jews were making a complaint about some misdemeanor or
serious crime, it would be reasonable for me to listen to you."
—ACTS 18:14 (NIV)

The happiness of your life depends upon the quality of your
thoughts: therefore, guard accordingly, and take care that you
entertain no notions unsuitable to virtue and reasonable nature.
— MARCUS AURELIUS

Dear Father, we are grateful for this day. Help us be reasonable
with our spending during this holiday season. Amen.

DECEMBER 8

Cheerful

Each of you should give what you have decided
in your heart to give, not reluctantly or under
compulsion, for God loves a cheerful giver.

—2 CORINTHIANS 9:7 (NIV)

The principles of living greatly include the capacity
to face trouble with courage, disappointment
with cheerfulness, and trial with humility.

—THOMAS S. MONSON

Dear God, let our words be pleasant. Let them bring cheer
and encouragement to others on this day. Amen.

Invigorate

When Jesus had called the Twelve together, he gave them power
and authority to drive out all demons and to cure diseases,
and he sent them out to proclaim the kingdom of God and to
heal the sick. He told them: "Take nothing for the journey—
no staff, no bag, no bread, no money, no extra shirt."
—LUKE 9:1–6 (NIV)

Don't you find that work, if you love it,
is actually really invigorating?
—CATE BLANCHETT

Dear God, thank you for this new day and the promises it
brings. Invigorate us today so we can know its blessings. Amen.

DECEMBER 10

God's Promises

For I tell you that Christ has become a servant of the
Jews on behalf of God's truth, so that the promises
made to the patriarchs might be confirmed.
—ROMANS 15:8 (NIV)

We have the promise of God's being our God, and of the
blessing by Christ for ourselves, as we are Abraham's seed, yet
take the whole promise collectively made to him and us.
—THOMAS GOODWIN

Dear God, you didn't say we wouldn't face challenges in
life, but you promised to be with us during them. Amen.

DECEMBER 11

Calm Spirit

A gentle answer turns away wrath, but a harsh word stirs up anger.
—PROVERBS 15:1 (NIV)

In the scriptures, "peace" means either freedom from strife,
contention, conflict, or war, or an inner calm and comfort
born of the Spirit that is a gift of God to all of his children,
an assurance and serenity within a person's heart.
—JOSEPH B. WIRTHLIN

Dear Father, we are grateful for this Friday. We are praying not
be anxious or fearful. Give us a calm, peaceful spirit. Amen.

DECEMBER 12

Bitterness

Get rid of all bitterness, rage and anger, brawling
and slander, along with every form of malice.

—EPHESIANS 4:31 (NIV)

Disappointment is inevitable. But to become discouraged,
there's a choice I make. God would never discourage me. He
would always point me to himself to trust him. Therefore,
my discouragement is from Satan. As you go through the
emotions that we have, hostility is not from God, bitterness,
un-forgiveness, all of these are attacks from Satan.

—CHARLES STANLEY

Dear Father, we thank you for this day. We are praying to get
over our past hurts and move forward free of bitterness. Amen.

DECEMBER 13

Fresh Anointing

As for you, the anointing you received from him remains in
you, and you do not need anyone to teach you. But as his
anointing teaches you about all things and as that anointing is
real, not counterfeit—just as it has taught you, remain in him.

—1 JOHN 2:27 (NIV)

The anointing, which is God's power, comes on
me … I can actually feel it. And people start getting
healed. From the cancer, the pain is gone.

—BENNY HINN

Dear God, we are praying for a fresh anointing of your Spirit, that
we may operate in excellence, power, and confidence. Amen.

DECEMBER 14

Shape or Future

For I know the plans I have for you," declares
the Lord, "plans to prosper you and not to harm
you, plans to give you hope and a future."
—JEREMIAH 29:11 (NIV)

The challenges of change are always hard. It is important that
we begin to unpack those challenges that confront this nation
and realize that we each have a role that requires us to change
and become more responsible for shaping our own future.
—HILLARY CLINTON

Thank you, Father, for this day. Yesterday is history, and tomorrow
a mystery. What we do today will help shape our future. Amen.

DECEMBER 15

Negativity

Righteousness exalts a nation, but sin condemns any people.
—PROVERBS 14:34 (NIV)

Experiencing sadness and anger can make you feel more creative,
and by being creative, you can get beyond your pain or negativity.
—YOKO ONO

Dear Father God, we thank you for another day. Please
help us stay focused on the positive things and not
allow negativity to have power over us. Amen.

DECEMBER 16

Procrastination

A sluggard's appetite is never filled, but the
desires of the diligent are fully satisfied.

—PROVERBS 13:4 (NIV)

Procrastination is the bad habit of putting off until the day after
tomorrow what should have been done the day before yesterday.

—NAPOLEON HILL

Dear Father, we are so grateful for another day among the living.
We are praying to make the best of this day and not procrastinate
or waste time on things that will not be productive. Amen.

DECEMBER 17

Open Mind
❧⟐❧

Open my eyes that I may see wonderful things in your law. I am a stranger on earth; do not hide your commands from me. My soul is consumed with longing for your laws at all times.

—PSALM 119:18–20 (NIV)

Despite my firm convictions, I have always been a man who tries to face facts, and to accept the reality of life as new experience and new knowledge unfolds. I have always kept an open mind, a flexibility that must go hand in hand with every form of the intelligent search for truth.

—MALCOLM X

Dear God, thank you for this day. Help us keep an open mind for the new and be creative in our thinking. Amen.

DECEMBER 18

Great Opportunities

If anyone, then, knows the good they ought to
do and doesn't do it, it is sin for them.
—JAMES 4:17 (NIV)

Don't wait for extraordinary opportunities. Seize
common occasions and make them great. Weak men
wait for opportunities; strong men make them.
—ORISON SWETT MARDEN

Dear God, prepare us for the opportunities that may present
themselves so that we may take full advantage of them. Amen.

DECEMBER 19

Maximize Productivity

Again, it will be like a man going on a journey, who called
his servants and entrusted his wealth to them. To one he
gave five bags of gold, to another two bags, and to another
one bag, each according to his ability. Then he went on his
journey. The man who had received five bags of gold went at
once and put his money to work and gained five bags more.

—MATTHEW 25:14–30 (NIV)

Productivity is never an accident. It is always
the result of a commitment to excellence,
intelligent planning, and focused effort.

—PAUL J. MEYER

Dear Father, we thank you for this day. We are praying to
prioritize our day in such a way to maximize productivity. Amen.

DECEMBER 20

Gifts and Talents

Again, it will be like a man going on a journey, who called
his servants and entrusted his wealth to them. To one he
gave five bags of gold, to another two bags, and to another
one bag, each according to his ability. Then he went on his
journey. The man who had received five bags of gold went at
once and put his money to work and gained five bags more.

—MATHEW 25:14–30 (NIV)

Talent is a gift which God has given us secretly,
and which we reveal without perceiving it.

—MONTESQUIEU

Dear Father, we are grateful for our gifts and talents. We
pray to use them to their fullest potential. Amen.

DECEMBER 21

Disobedience

In which you used to live when you followed the ways of
this world and of the ruler of the kingdom of the air, the
spirit who is now at work in those who are disobedient.

—EPHESIANS 2:2 (NIV)

Disobedience is essentially a prideful power struggle against
someone in authority over us. It can be a parent, a priesthood
leader, a teacher, or ultimately God. A proud person hates the fact
that someone is above him. He thinks this lowers his position.

— EZRA TAFT BENSON

Dear Father, we are praying not to block our blessings because
of our disobedience and unforgiveness in our hearts. Amen.

DECEMBER 22

Victory

Moses replied: "It is not the sound of victory, it is not the sound of defeat; it is the sound of singing that I hear."

—EXODUS 32:18 (NIV)

Peace is the beauty of life. It is sunshine. It is the smile of a child, the love of a mother, the joy of a father, the togetherness of a family. It is the advancement of man, the victory of a just cause, the triumph of truth.

—MENACHEM BEGIN

Dear Father, we thank you for this day. We are praying for a closer walk with you, claiming victory over all negativity. Amen.

DECEMBER 23

Impact

❧⁓❧

As for those who were held in high esteem—whatever
they were makes no difference to me; God does not show
favoritism—they added nothing to my message.

—GALATIANS 2:6 (NIV)

In every day, there are 1,440 minutes. That means we have
1,440 daily opportunities to make a positive impact.

—LES BROWN

Father, thank you for this day. Help us be directional, be
productive, and make an impact—and not just shadowbox. Amen.

DECEMBER 24

Mismanage

For God is not a God of disorder but of peace—as
in all the congregations of the Lord's people.
—1 CORINTHIANS 14:33 (NIV)

We all can do our part to address America's anger
mismanagement crisis. And for us Christians, it
starts with a little more faith, hope, and love.
—ERIC METAXAS

Dear Father, thank you for this day. We are praying not to
mismanage our faith and let your will be done in our lives. Amen.

DECEMBER 25

Joy

But the fruit of the Spirit is love, joy, peace,
forbearance, kindness, goodness, faithfulness.
—GALATIANS 5:22 (NIV)

I write about the power of trying, because I want to be
okay with failing. I write about generosity because I battle
selfishness. I write about joy because I know sorrow. I
write about faith because I almost lost mine, and I know
what it is to be broken and in need of redemption. I write
about gratitude because I am thankful—for all of it.
—KRISTIN ARMSTRONG

Dear God, we are praying to stop expecting
people, places, and things to give us the joy that
comes only through your Spirit. Amen.

DECEMBER 26

God's Spirit

And hope does not put us to shame, because God's
love has been poured out into our hearts through
the Holy Spirit, who has been given to us.

—ROMANS 5:5 (NIV)

All that men will serve God with must be done in Faith, viz.
in the Spirit. It is the Spirit that maketh the work perfect, and
acceptable in the sight of God. All that a man undertaketh and
doeth in Faith, he doth in the Spirit of God, which Spirit of God
doth co-operate in the work, and then it is acceptable to God.

—JAKOB BOHME

Dear God, we thank you for a conscious contact with you. Fill us
with your Spirit—and give us purpose and direction today. Amen.

DECEMBER 27

Create

Create in me a pure heart, O God, and
renew a steadfast spirit within me.
—PSALM 51:10 (NIV)

Your personal life, your professional life, and your creative life are
all intertwined. I went through a few very difficult years where I
felt like a failure. But it was actually really important for me to go
through that. Struggle, for me, is the most inspirational thing in
the world at the end of the day—as long as you treat it that way.
—SKYLAR GREY

Dear God, we are grateful for this day. We are
praying to be positive and creative. We are grateful
for living this life to its fullest. Amen.

DECEMBER 28

Anxiousness

Do not be anxious about anything, but in
every situation, by prayer and petition, with
thanksgiving, present your requests to God.

—PHILIPPIANS 4:6 (NIV)

I get anxious about a lot of things, that's the trouble.
I get anxious about everything. I just can't stop
thinking about things all the time. And here's the really
destructive part—it's always retrospective. I waste time
thinking of what I should have said or done.

—HUGH LAURIE

Dear Father, we are praying not to be anxious or fearful—and to
walk in the boldness and confidence you have given us. Amen.

Good Character

Do not be misled: "Bad company corrupts good character."
—1 CORINTHIANS 15:33 (NIV)

Good character is not formed in a week or a month.
It is created little by little, day by day. Protracted and
patient effort is needed to develop good character.
—HERACLITUS

Dear Father, we are grateful for this day. We are praying to be
our very best on this day, allowing you to guide us. Amen.

DECEMBER 30

Prejudices

Joseph had a dream, and when he told it to his
brothers, they hated him all the more.
—GENESIS 37:5 (NIV)

Prejudices, it is well known, are most difficult to eradicate from
the heart whose soil has never been loosened or fertilized by
education; they grow firm there, firm as weeds among stones.
—CHARLOTTE BRONTË

Dear Father, help us with traditionalism and any prejudices that
hinder our spiritual growth and block our blessings. Amen.

DECEMBER 31

Move Forward

"Get out of our way," they replied. "This fellow came here
as a foreigner, and now he wants to play the judge! We'll
treat you worse than them." They kept bringing pressure
on Lot and moved forward to break down the door.
—GENESIS 19:9 (NIV)

Even though you may want to move forward in your life, you may
have one foot on the brakes. In order to be free, we must learn how
to let go. Release the hurt. Release the fear. Refuse to entertain
your old pain. The energy it takes to hang onto the past is holding
you back from a new life. What is it you would let go of today?
—MARY MANIN MORRISSEY

Dear Father, thank you for this day. We are praying to move
forward in life and stop reliving the pain of the past. Amen.

Printed in the United States
By Bookmasters